SMOLLETT
AND THE SCOTTISH SCHOOL

SMOLLETT

AND THE

SCOTTISH SCHOOL

STUDIES IN

EIGHTEENTH-CENTURY THOUGHT

M. A. GOLDBERG

ALBUQUERQUE

UNIVERSITY OF NEW MEXICO PRESS

FOR EARL R. WASSERMAN
Inter sylvas Academi quaerere verum.

CONTENTS

ACKNOWLEDGEMENTS are made to the Ford Foundation, whose grant made possible the publication of the text; to the University of New Mexico for grants-in-aid which allowed for revision of the manuscript; to the Journal of Aesthetics and Art Criticism *for permission to reprint a section of Chapter Three, which originally appeared in its pages; to Professor E. R. Wasserman of The Johns Hopkins University for his invaluable assistance, his vigorous criticism, and his careful readings of the manuscript; to Professors Charles R. Anderson, Georges Poulet, and C. V. Wicker for kind and helpful suggestions; to Dr. Owsei Temkin for his assistance with a section of Chapter Five; to Professor Leo Spitzer for his assistance with some of Chapter Four; and to my wife and to the many friends who read, typed, argued, harangued, pleaded, cajoled, and in general made possible or impossible the text in its present form.*

PREFACE

THE SUCCEEDING CHAPTERS propose an examination of Smollett's novels against the background of ideas current in the eighteenth century, particularly those emanating from the Scottish Common-Sense School, with which the novelist had many affiliations. This is not to imply that Smollett is a philosophical writer, or that the end of his novels (or indeed, the end of any work of art) is necessarily intellectual or ideational. But art exists within an attitudinal frame, from which its symbols are derived and through which its form achieves meaning. We turn to an historical dictionary for word-meanings which have shifted in time. With much the same intent, I have turned to the eighteenth-century Scots for ideational meanings which have shifted or become obsolete. Not that Scottish tradition provides a *raison d'être* for the novels, but tradition can illuminate the complexity of structure and reveal perhaps more readily and more clearly thematic developments within Smollett.

There is, I believe, much justification for this approach. In his preface to *Roderick Random* the novelist proposes to imitate Cervantes in aiming at purposes "useful and entertaining" and to "point out the follies of ordinary life," while in his preface to *Ferdinand Count Fathom* he announces his intention "to instruct the ignorant, and entertain the vacant . . . to subject folly to ridicule, and vice to indignation." His use of satire, however, differs from that of Cervantes and Le Sage, as Smollett himself points out in his preface. Of course it also differs from Erasmus' techniques in attacking folly

during the Renaissance and from Thackeray's, during the nine-
teenth century. Smollett's aims have more in common with the tradition emerging out of the ethical and esthetic strictures of the
Scottish Common-Sense School.

Tradition, of course, is multi-faceted. Louis L. Martz's admirable volume, examining Smollett in the eighteenth-century tradition of editing and compiling, is one approach to the novelist.
George M. Kahrl's examination of Smollett in the tradition of travel
literature is yet another. One could well place Smollett against the
background of the Spanish *pícaro* or that of the Scottish satirists,
Henryson and Dunbar. These approaches are not mutually exclu-
sive, however, and my emphasis throughout upon Smollett's philosophical assumptions and his ethical views is scarcely intended to
imply this.

For some time now, eighteenth-century English tradition has
been rigidly defined as an age of contention over a series of concepts
seemingly antithetical. In this study it is held that Smollett—like the
forty-odd rhetoricians, estheticians, moral philosophers, social
and cultural historians comprising the Scottish Common-Sense
School—held to neither side of the controversy, but maintained a
middle-ground, experiential in method, ethical in end, insistent
upon a "common-sense" reconciliation of the standard contrarieties
of the age.

The antithesis of reason and passion is examined in *Roderick
Random*; art and nature in *Ferdinand Count Fathom*; imagination
and judgment in *Peregrine Pickle*; benevolence and self-love in *Sir
Launcelot Greaves*; and primitivism and the idea of progress in
Humphry Clinker. It would certainly be a distortion to insist that
any single problem to the exclusion of others is localized within a
particular novel. In each case, I have simply unraveled one essential
thread, attempting to lay bare an important nexus for the work.

Since words, as well as ideas, have altered in time, I have attempted whenever possible to remain close to Smollett's original lan-

guage without wrenching apart the symbolic threads from which the web of adventure is spun. The frequent references to the novels have been taken from George Saintsbury's twelve-volume edition of *The Works of Tobias Smollett* (London, n.d.). Allusions to volume and page, as they appear within my text, are to this edition.

M. A. GOLDBERG

Yellow Springs, Ohio
January, 1959

[Titles of learned and critical journals generally are abbreviated in the notes as follows: *ELH, English Literary History; JAAC, Journal of Aesthetics and Art Criticism; JEGP, Journal of English and Germanic Philology; MLN, Modern Language Notes; MP, Modern Philology; PMLA, Publication of the Modern Language Association; PQ, Philological Quarterly; VS, Victorian Studies.*]

CHAPTER ONE. *SMOLLETT*

and the Scottish Common-Sense School

1₀ TOBIAS GEORGE SMOLLETT is still regarded as a major eighteenth-century novelist, despite the decline in his literary reputation over the past hundred-and-fifty years. Typical of the ambiguities surrounding the Scottish writer, that reputation now rests almost entirely on one book, *Humphry Clinker.* Strangely, critics have never found much to say in attesting to its greatness. For the most part, they have restricted themselves to comments about its humor or its realism, or about biographical implications.

Hazlitt's remark about *Humphry Clinker,* that this is "the most pleasant gossiping novel that ever was written," appears to have set the dictates for over a century of literary criticism. Since Hazlitt, critics have been content to mull over some of the gossip —the description of Bath, the oddity of Lismahago, the petulance of Bramble—as if this were the *causa sine qua non* for the novel's greatness.

This vagueness surrounding Smollett's novels has precipitated a host of ambiguities. Two recent and antithetical attitudes are typical: one suggests Smollett as traveler, whose diverse itineraries formed some basis for this last novel; the other, Smollett as editor and compiler, supplied with vicarious adventures through his extensive readings.[1] Studies of biography or of sources and analogues can certainly provide a mode by which the work of art may be holistically seen. Too frequently, however, the mode is confused with the art, the part confused with the whole. Almost invariably, this has been the case in examining Smollett and the eighteenth-century novelists in general.

These antithetical portraits of Smollett as sedentary editor and as nomadic traveler are typical. Studies of the novelist abound with ambiguities and contradictions. One group, for example, portrays Smollett as a man of intellectual breadth. Alexander Carlyle, an intimate friend of the novelist, recalls in his *Autobiography* that Smollett "possessed a philosophical mind, and was capable of making the soundest observations on human life." This view is sustained by many of the novelist's contemporaries, though few have gone so far as one modern writer, who has detected in Smollett's nautical characterizations a stoicism paralleling that of early Church writers and philosophers. Diametrically opposed to this view, however, is Hazlitt's contention that Smollett "seldom probes to the quick, or penetrates beyond the surface." Since Hazlitt, most critics have dismissed the novelist as a trivial humorist, unconcerned with the subtle ironies and deeper ambiguities of life.[2]

Ambiguities also surround the writer's sentimentalism. Coleridge remarks on "the congeniality of humor with pathos, so exquisite in . . . Smollett." Following Coleridge, several modern critics have discerned romantic scenes in both *Humphry Clinker* and *Ferdinand Count Fathom* and concluded that Smollett was aiming at sentimental effects. On the other hand, Smollett has frequently been identified with the realism of Defoe and Hogarth and alternately applauded or indicted for his lack of sentiment, for his callousness and brutality.[3]

Another major ambiguity surrounds Smollett's humanitarianism. The *Critical Review* for 1762 found indications of Smollett's benevolent heart in *Sir Launcelot Greaves*. A recent biographical study also comments on "Smollett's warm and generous instincts" and observes that "in his extreme generosity Smollett was obviously the man of feeling." However, Lawrence Sterne satirically portrays Smollett in *A Sentimental Journey* as the truculent and misanthropic Smelfungus. Sterne's satire is scarcely arbitrary, since the

Scottish novelist has often been condemned for depicting his own dyspeptic malevolence, a world of spite, contempt and uncharitableness.[4]

Smollett's political position is equally ambiguous and contradictory. Sir Walter Scott discerns in the *History* an announcement of political principles, "those of a moderate Tory, and a favourer of the monarchical part of our constitution." Alexander Carlyle, a close friend of Smollett who should have known his political leanings, writes also that the Scotchman was a Tory, though not a Jacobite. On the other hand, some see the novelist as a Whig; others as a Whig who followed in his youth the principles of the party in which he had been educated, but who changed allegiances, following the Whig's harsh policy toward Scotland after the rebellion of 1745. Still, the *Critical Review* for 1758 observes in the *History* "incontrovertible proofs of the author's impartiality. Attached to no party, and independent of both, he scorned to suppress any circumstance tending to the illustration of historical truth." Smollett himself, in a letter to William Huggins, writes of the *History*: "I have kept myself independent of all Connexions which might have affected the Candour of my Intention. I have flattered no Individual: I have cultivated no Party."[5]

Clearly, then, we are presented with a rather confused series of antitheses surrounding Smollett. He is both philosophical and a trivial humorist; a man of sentiment, and also a hardened realist; a benevolent humanitarian, but also an encrusted misanthrope; an aristocratic Tory, but simultaneously a plebeian Whig. Part of this confusion, no doubt, results from our own shifting standards of taste. Lewis Knapp's recent biography, however, admits the validity of these antithetical forces in the Scottish writer:

> There were in Smollett, as in many other dynamic and complex personalities, two powerful forces, at times mutually antagonistic, but, in the long run, essentially interlocking and complementary. In many respects Smollett aspired to be, and was, a typical rationalist, a typical satirist, and a conventionally aristocratic gentleman of the mideighteenth century. At the same time, he was, in many respects, a

man of ebullient and violent feelings which often escaped from the
leash of reason; a person repeatedly unconventional for his times in
romantic self-confession; and a very generous humanitarian.[6]

This portrayal of a dichotomous and dual-natured Smollett appears
judicious and fairly objective. Yet, we cannot hope to gain much
of an insight into the mind of Smollett, the force that lies behind
the novels and gives them their form, unless we see in a rather precise way how these antithetical qualities become "essentially interlocking and complementary." Conceivably, scholarship on Smollett
has taken its present form *because* of these contradictions: avoiding
ambiguities by dismissing them as typically picaresque; or attempting to solve the ambiguities by delving into the biographical.
In either event, the novels themselves have received only cursory
examination.

If we admit the presence of these "mutually antagonistic"
forces in Smollett, then we must also admit the anomaly of finding
them in an eighteenth-century figure. This was an age when individuals were rabidly partisan in their affiliations. It has become
almost a commonplace to analyze the eighteenth century in England as an intellectual battleground, torn with oppositions of every
kind: political, religious, esthetic, literary, horticultural, metaphysical. Political historians interpret the struggle as one between
declining Toryism and ascendant Whiggism. Literary critics generally detect a major conflict between "neo-classicism" and "sentimentalism" or "romanticism." Arthur O. Lovejoy describes the age
as an opposition between uniformitarianism and diversitarianism;
Ronald S. Crane, as a struggle between rules or first principles and
spontaneity or sublimity; Lois Whitney, as a constant altercation
between primitivism and the idea of progress; Walter Jackson Bate,
as the retreat of rationalism against the rapid incursion of empiricism and intuitionalism.[7] In any event, though perspectives differ,
critics have almost unanimously seen this as an age of irreconcilable
faction and sharp dichotomy. In eighteenth-century England one
was either Whig or Tory; for a developing middle class or for a

declining aristocracy; for a rising cult of feeling or for a deterio-
rating set of rules or first principles; an adherent of progress toward
perfectibility or a believer in the superior greatness of the ancients.

In any examination of Smollett as an eighteenth-century
writer, therefore, we face a particular kind of dilemma. Either our
conception of eighteenth-century controversies is a valid one, in
which case the picture of Smollett who adheres to both sides of the
conflict is erroneous; or our picture of Smollett is valid, in which
case the controversies of the century were not as irreconcilable and
dichotomous as we might believe.

As revealed through his novels, however, Smollett is neither
ambiguous nor contradictory. Forces antithetical for most of the
century appear in Smollett truly complementary and interlocking,
so that the novelist emerges as an understandable, integrated representative of his age. Just as Smollett was capable of reconciling the
standard contrarieties of the eighteenth century, a large segment of
the period was also capable of reconciliations, literary as well as
philosophical. Mainly, this was possible through the influence of
the Scottish Common-Sense School.

2. SMOLLETT'S RELATIONSHIP with the Scottish Common-Sense School is personal and cultural, as well as intellectual.
Born in 1721 at Dalquhurn, near Bonhill, Dumbartonshire, the
novelist was descended from an ancestry devoted to Scottish law and
military affairs. His early, formative years were spent in the midst of
an active period of fermentation for Scotland—between the crucial
Treaty of Union in 1707, when the country merged politically with
England, and the Jacobite rebellions in 1745-46, after which it
became clear that Scotland's future was irrevocably tied with that
of England. Although documented facts for Smollett's early life
are few, his recent biographer offers a plausible reconstruction of
the years of study. About 1727 or 1728 he entered Dumbarton
grammar school, remaining probably some five years. His stay at

Glasgow University can only be tentatively fixed, since his name is
absent from matriculation albums, and since he failed to graduate;
however, evidence dates his enrollment between 1735 and 1739,
during which time it seems probable that he came under the influence of Francis Hutcheson, Professor of Moral Philosophy. It is
quite plausible that he might also have known, during his final year
at Glasgow University, Adam Smith, the economist, who was in
residence at that time.[8]

Although Smollett left Scotland for London when he was
eighteen, returning only for infrequent visits, his allegiance re-
mained unswervingly with the North. This constant identification
with Scot tradition is apparent in "The Tears of Scotland" (1746),
a spirited protest against England's celebration of her victory at
Culloden; in *Roderick Random*, whose Scot-loving hero is invari-
ably identified with the novelist himself; and in a book as late as
Humphry Clinker, usually seen as a slashing denunciation of the
English and a spirited exaltation of the Scots. Even the *Critical
Review*, which Smollett edited from 1756 to 1763, has been labeled
a "Scotch Tribunal," with Smollett excoriated as its head, by
Thomas Shebbeare in *The Occasional Critic, or the Decrees of the
Scotch Tribunal in the Critical Rejudged* (1757) and again in an
Appendix to the Occasional Critic, which pointed to the prejudice
of the *Critical Review* in favor of Scottish writers. Almost invari-
ably, eighteenth-century writers alluded to the magazine as a
"Scotch" organ. Significantly, Smollett himself expresses this
affinity for Scotland in his letter to Carlyle (1754):

> I do not think I could enjoy life with greater relish in any part of the
> World than in Scotland among you and your friends, and I often
> amuse my imagination with schemes for attaining that degree of
> happiness, which however is altogether out of my reach—I am heartily
> tired of this land of indifference and phlegm where the finer sensa-
> tions of the soul are not felt . . . Where Genius is lost, learning
> undervalued, Taste altogether extinguished, and Ignorance prevail.

It is certainly possible to justify Smollett's ardent Scottish
fervor when considering the animosity of eighteenth-century Lon-

doners to their northern neighbors, a factor which must have
limited the novelist's social activities and prevented any full identification of self with England.[9] Though this may have operated in
part, there were certainly positive and more obvious reasons behind
Smollett's consistent identification with Scottish tradition. True,
the Jacobites had suffered a military defeat at Culloden in '45, but
Scotland emerged almost at once to compensate for its humiliation
with an intellectual surge which has been compared with a similar
movement during the Age of Pericles. Within a brief period Scotland's "Golden Age" had produced a major philosopher, David
Hume; the historian, William Robertson; poet Robert Burns; novelists Smollett and Scott; biographers Boswell and Lockhart. Adam
Smith was achieving world fame as an economist; James Watt, for
his engineering feats; Joseph Black, with chemistry; James Hutton,
in geology; William Cullen and John Hunter, for their studies in
pathology. As early as 1757, before most of these figures had reached
their heights, David Hume was writing Gilbert Elliot of Minto
about the strange forces at work in Scotland:

> Is it not strange that, at a time when we have lost our Princes, our
> Parliaments, our independent Government, even the Presence of our
> chief Nobility . . . is it not strange, I say, that in these Circum-
> stances, we shou'd really be the People most distinguish'd for Liter-
> ture in Europe?

Smollett appears to have enjoyed some degree of intimacy with
most of the Scottish literary lights. It is usually assumed that the
Edinburgh letters of July 18 and August 8 in *Humphry Clinker*
contain much that is autobiographical, and that Smollett was well
acquainted with the "hot-bed of genius" which Matthew Bramble
lists there, including David Hume, John Home, William Robertson, Adam Smith, Robert Wallace, Hugh Blair, William Wilkie,
and Adam Ferguson.

We can only conjecture as to the validity of the autobiographical in *Humphry Clinker*, but we can state with reasonable assurance
and despite the paucity of actual biographical evidence that Smollett was well within this "hot-bed of genius." True, only a single

letter to David Hume is extant among Smollett's correspondence, but in it the novelist alludes to "friendly intercourse" with Hume, whose own correspondence confirms this friendship. In addition, the intimacy Smollett enjoyed with Dr. Alexander Carlyle, recorded in Bramble's letter of August 8, is confirmed, partially by Carlyle's many allusions to Smollett throughout his *Autobiography*, but also by ten letters from Smollett to Carlyle which have survived. We know from these same sources that through Carlyle Smollett developed a friendship for William Robertson, the historian. And through Carlyle, Smollett undoubtedly met Adam Smith, Hugh Blair, Adam Ferguson, and the other luminaries with whom Carlyle was intimately acquainted—unless Smollett already knew these men through other channels. It is inconceivable, given the reputation Smollett had, particularly during his last years, and given the closely-knit Scot society in London, as Carlyle pictures it, that these men should not seek Smollett out, or that he should not have sought out their company.

It is less than relevant to wonder whether Smollett actually read the works of the Scottish group, or whether conversations with them were of an intellectual nature. It is sufficient to note that he emerged from the same forces erupting in Scotland which produced an Adam Smith, a Hugh Blair, or an Adam Ferguson—that he clung to Scottish tradition, partly from necessity, as a member of a minority group; partly from desire, because this was where his affiliations lay. Of still greater import is that ideas expressed in Smollett's major works—by direct statement of thought and intention, by interaction of characters, by the development of architectonics—are paralleled most closely by the Scottish Common-Sense School.

3. IN A RECENT SURVEY of ideational currents in eighteenth-century England, A. S. P. Woodhouse suggests the possibility of a mediating role for the Scottish group relative to major intellec-

tual movements. Of four schools or traditions distinguishable in the eighteenth century, Woodhouse explains, one was the thorough system of materialism, stemming from Hobbes and providing a mechanistic conception of nature and mind. Another was the dominant tradition of empiricism, initiated by Locke and fully developed in Hume, isolating the mind and concentrating instead upon impressions and ideas. These two schools later merged under the mechanistic impetus of the associational psychologists. A third tradition, rationalism, an outgrowth of the seventeenth-century Cambridge Platonists, whose ideas were promulgated in the following century by Shaftesbury, Clarke, Price and Godwin, insisted on the validity of reason in uncovering the true source for knowledge, independent of sensation. But there was yet another tradition, Woodhouse asserts:

> The fourth tradition—that of the Scottish Common-Sense School —represents an effort of compromise between rationalism and empiricism: its aims have much in common with the former, its methods with the latter, whose interest in psychology it shared to the full. And herein lay its chief importance for literature, since most of the Scottish writers who were reshaping the critical theory of the eighteenth century either came under the influence of, or at least shared the interests manifested by, the Common-Sense School.[10]

Initiated by Francis Hutcheson, and achieving a major impetus through Thomas Reid, the Common-Sense School represents an effort, singular until the last decades, in reconciling a dualism inherent in Western thought since the close of the seventeenth century. Then, as Alfred North Whitehead has pointed out, knowledge was split into two discernible areas, that of materialistic nature and that of cogitating minds, with philosophy assuming charge of the latter, science of the former. "The objective world of science was confined to mere spatial material with simple location in space and time, and subjected to definite rules as to its locomotion," Whitehead affirms. "The subjective world of philosophy annexed the colours, sounds, scents, tastes, touches, bodily feelings, as forming the subjective content of the cogitations of the individual minds." Because most philosophers have examined the English empirical movement relative only to its more fruitful development in Kant and the German idealists, they have tended to see in the Scottish movement only a temporary diversion of current lines of thought, which thrust the philosophical impulse into a side track and initiated a decline of speculative force. From the perspective of twentieth-century thought, however, "the whole of the great German idealistic movement will be ignored [by modern philosophy], as being out of effective touch with its contemporary science so far as reciprocal modification of concepts is concerned," if we assume the broader vision Whitehead projects in *Science and the Modern World*. The more limited perspective, it would seem, misjudges the significance and intentions of the Scottish group, even while soundly appraising its limitations, for the School was truly inadequate to the challenge which it faced and proved incapable of managing its inheritance.[11]

Although Thomas Reid is generally considered the outstanding proponent of the Scottish School, he is scarcely its most representative figure. Because his concern with writing a direct refutation of Hume involved him with the language of empiricism, itself inherently antithetical to the common-sense philosophy he was propounding, much of the actual nature of Reid's contentions is obscured. Confining himself almost exclusively to an investigation of the "intellectual" and "active" powers of man, Reid tends to ignore social, ethical, and cultural aspects of the common-sense philosophy which were basic to the thinking of the entire group and which allowed it to bridge the gap between the rationalists and the mechanism of the later empiricists.

Among the forty-odd moral and social philosophers, cultural historians, rhetoricians, critics, and estheticians forming the nucleus of the Scottish School, Adam Ferguson, frequently called "the founder of modern sociology," is without doubt most representative. Ferguson's *Essay on the History of Civil Society* (1767), especially the First Part which treats "Of the General Characteristics of Human Nature," reveals with clarity a view shared by almost the whole group. Here, within ten sub-sections, Ferguson lays down the method, terminology, and assumptions which form the basis of the history proper.[12]

The first section of Ferguson's *Essay*, like Smollett's *Ferdinand Count Fathom*, concerns itself with a typical eighteenth-century opposition, the antithesis of art and nature. Like Smollett, Ferguson sees this antagonism as false and artificial, contrary to the dicta of experience and common sense. Most poets, historians, and moralists, in examining the early stages of society, have assumed an initial state of nature from which mankind has either degenerated or improved; however, this is the result more of conjecture than of fact, Ferguson observes, and has led to ill-founded theories about art and society being an improvement upon or a degeneration from this original state of nature. Impartial observation, however, reveals that man now, as always, subsists in groups. If a pre-social state once existed, then we have no record of it; as far as we know empirically, society is perfectly natural to man. Thus, Ferguson points out, "we speak of art as distinguished from nature; but art itself is natural to man," and in no situation of the human race, as we know it, is art unknown:

> If we admit that man is susceptible of improvement, and has in himself a principle of progression, and a desire of perfection, it appears improper to say, that he has quitted the state of nature, when he has begun to proceed; or that he finds a station for which he was not intended, while, like other animals, he only follows the disposition, and employs the powers that nature has given.

Accordingly, Ferguson insists, in human affairs the terms "*natural* and *unnatural* are the least determinate in their meaning [and] . . . can serve to distinguish nothing: for all the actions of men are equally the result of their nature." Instead of seeking to distinguish between art and nature, therefore, we ought to distinguish between justice and injustice, happiness and wretchedness, for it is more important to learn the condition toward which we should aspire, granted our own nature, rather than to study the state which mankind may be supposed to have left.

Similarly, the position Smollett adopts toward benevolence and self-love in *The Adventures of Sir Launcelot Greaves* is paralleled closely in the second section of Ferguson's text. Writers have disputed about man's innate selfishness or man's innate altruism, Ferguson explains, but here too are theories which are more imaginary than real. Experience shows us that man has instinctive propensities leading him "to perform many functions which terminate in himself, or have a relation to his fellow-creatures. He has one set of dispositions which tend to his animal preservation, and . . . another which lead to society." To call either disposition *self-love* is erroneous, Ferguson contends. The term *interest* is perhaps more appropriate, for it is no less to our interest to satisfy our need to be loved than it is to satisfy our appetite for food. Distinctions ought to be ethical, and based on human action rather than on conjectured propensities; thus, we ought "to distinguish the humane from the cruel, and the benevolent from the selfish."

In the same vein, Ferguson points out in his third and fourth sections that different writers have argued that either war or amity is the state of nature; and that men unite through principles of affection, or through principles of fear. History, however, reveals that men "are to one another mutual objects both of fear and of love." Everywhere, man has enemies as well as friends; besides, generosity and self-denial can be the cause of friendship and amity, but also they can cause hostility and warfare, for friendship to one may serve as a threat to another.

Yet another conflict, the opposition between passion and reason, crucial to *The Adventures of Roderick Random*, is the subject of Ferguson's fifth section. Some contend that man is a rational creature, while others contend that he is ruled by his passions. But man's disposition consists of both passions and reason, Ferguson insists. "One great accomplishment of the living agent consists in the force and sensibility of his animal organs"; but the relationship between the objects around us which we discern is also subject to "faculties of penetration and judgment." Neither sensibility nor judgment is in itself a good. Though the Romans were more knowing than the Greeks, and modern scholars are more learned than either Greeks or Romans, superiority lies not in what men know, but in what they do, it is contended. In moral actions among men, "the understanding appears to borrow very much from the passions"; and where the "promptitude of the head" is united with "ardour and sensibility of the heart," we are confronted with "that superiority of mind [which] . . . should determine the rate of their genius, and assign the palm of distinction and honour."

Sections six to eight in Ferguson's *Essay* also strive for a medial and common-sense position toward a conventional eighteenth-century antithesis. Some, in concerning themselves with moral sentiment, would find "profit or loss" marking the event of all transactions, and would employ "the epithets *useful* or *detrimental*" in distinguishing men; but common sense reveals that these terms scarcely account for the great sentiments of the human heart, Ferguson explains. "Characters of men, not their situations and fortunes, are the principal distinction." Others would use the "terms *pleasure* and *pain*," but these are also equivocal in comprehending all the constituents of happiness or misery. Mere animal pleasures can turn to satiety and disgust. Happiness rather depends upon the employment of our talents, the materials with which we are furnished.

> The division of our appetites into benevolent and selfish, has probably, in some degree, helped to mislead our apprehension on the subject of personal enjoyment and private good. . . . In reality, the gratification of every desire is a personal enjoyment, . . . its value being proportioned to the particular quality or force of the sentiment.

Again, in the two concluding sections, Ferguson offers a basic reconciliation of oppositions typical of the age. There are those who would hold that either a democracy or an aristocracy is a perfect form of government, or that interests of individuals or interests of society are of greater importance. "The interests of society, however, and of its members, are easily reconciled," Ferguson explains. Though the individual must consider the state, he receives in turn the greatest happiness of which his nature is capable. Since men possess different powers and talents, and since national felicity is derived not from wealth or multitude but from the character of people, who differ one from the other, and from one time to the next, it is impossible to discern any single political form that would suit mankind in every condition. On the contrary, states rise and fall, as the characters of their people change; and though "democracy and despotism appear to be the opposite extremes at which constitutions of government farthest recede from one another," yet these societies can easily pass from one condition to the next.

Having established his common-sense prospectus of human nature, through a reconciliation, linguistic in manner, ethical in end, of the basic antitheses of the century, Ferguson proceeds in the succeeding sections of his *Essay* to a discussion of the *differentiae* apparent in the history of nations—property, talent, population, climate—all conducive to rise and decline.

The success of Ferguson's work at home and abroad was almost immediate. It went through seven editions during his lifetime, and was soon translated into German and French. Hume and d'Holbach acclaimed its genius; Adam Smith regarded the author as an important rival; William Robertson alluded to the text with frequency in his *History*; and Dugald Stewart saw himself as a follower and exponent.

A. S. P. Woodhouse is not alone in viewing the Scottish writers in general as a reconciling movement between antithetical forces. In an extended analysis of sociological currents during the eighteenth century, Gladys Bryson makes almost the same observation:

> The century was absorbed in procedures, conventions, arrangements; at the same time it was concerned with the spontaneous, the pre-conventional, the natural. The bridge which it made between the two sets of apparently antithetic concepts was the belief that it was natural for man to make an order of life different from that in which the race was nurtured earlier, that it was in the nature of his equipment that it should react intelligently and creatively to the situations in which he found himself, however new and different and difficult they might be.[13]

Roy Harvey Pearce, too, develops at length the reconciliations which the Scottish School afforded, enabling it to see, despite the common currents of opinion, that primitivism carried with it both virtues and defects, as did civilized life:

> It was their writing from a relativistic, historical point of view which enabled them to account for primitive nobility and Homer and Ossian and which at the same time enabled them satisfactorily to explain just why they could not have great heroes and great poets in their time. Further, they were enabled to explain why they would not want such heroes and such poets. . . . Perhaps all this is most significant as another aspect of the romantic proclivities of an essentially conservative, self-satisfied eighteenth-century society. . . . A single romantic tendency—an interest in the far away and simple—somehow fitted into a neo-classic life-view and thus became safely non-romantic.[14]

Whereas Pearce's study attempts to understand the Scottish group through its own terms, its "relativistic, historical point of view," another and more typical study by Lois Whitney eyes the Scottish writers from the perspective of dominant English currents and finds them violating their own sense of logic. Because an irreconcilable dichotomy of sensibility and rationalism is assumed initially, the Scottish effort at *rapprochement* necessarily appears puerile and inconsistent. Accordingly, Lord Kames is condemned for his attempts "to hold to the theories of primitivism and progressivism at the same time." Monboddo, whose "solution is even more ingenious than that of Kames," is roundly chastised for his efforts to "reconcile the idea of progress with the theory of progressive degeneration."[15]

Whitney's bemused treatment of Kames and Monboddo, like her condemnation of many of the minor novelists of the period who juxtapose ideas of sensibility and rationalism with small discrimination, points to a problem central to any analysis of Smollett. If we assume a basic dichotomy between art and nature, reason and feeling, primitivism and progress, benevolence and self-love—as many historians of ideas tend to do—then a great many works within the century must appear trivial, illogical, insignificant, and, as with Smollett, somewhat contradictory and ambiguous. If, on the other hand, we consider the middle ground which Ferguson and the Scottish writers seem to afford, and examine these works relative only to their own assumptions, then much that has appeared trivial may become in turn significant, and much that has appeared ambiguous and contradictory may become lucid and harmonious.

4. SMOLLETT, THEN, offers a subject most fruitful for analysis: because of his apparent contradictory nature; and because of his obvious affiliations with the Scottish Common-Sense School, which set out to bridge the major contradictions of the eighteenth century.

One basic assumption underlying all of Smollett's novels involves the antipodal nature of man. This is outlined most clearly in *Ferdinand Count Fathom*, where the author lays down his thesis that men are both selfish and social, and that egotism and hostilities are just "as universal, if not as natural" as benevolence and harmony. Assuming a medial position in a controversy crucial to his times, Smollett is ostensibly placing himself in opposition to followers of Hobbes and Mandeville, who were expounding theories of man's innate selfishness, and to the Cambridge Platonists, who were promulgating notions about man's innate benevolence. With obvious reference to the Cambridge Platonists and Shaftesbury, Smollett observes that whereas "a disciple of Plato, and some modern moralists" would attribute successful human action "to the innate virtue and generosity of the human heart, which naturally espouses the cause that needs protection," he himself has yet another view:

> I, whose notions of human excellence are not quite so sublime, am apt to believe it is owing to that spirit of self-conceit and contradiction,

which is, at least, as universal, if not as natural, as the moral sense so
warmly contended for by those ideal philosophers.   (II, 116-17)

Consequently, the universe Smollett constructs within his novels is
formed equally of both elements, the "spirit of self-conceit and
contradiction," but also the "innate virtue and generosity of the
human heart." Thus, the rogue-hero in *Ferdinand Count Fathom*
pits himself equally against two sets of antagonists: fellow-rogues
who, like him, are motivated by selfishness and appetites; but also
creatures of sensibility who display humaneness and benevolence.
Similarly, though Roderick Random is constantly indignant at the
"selfishness, envy, malice, and base indifference of mankind," he is
ever aware of the generosity and virtues of Strap, Narcissa, and
Tom Bowling. From the very beginning, Peregrine Pickle faces the
humaneness of the Trunnions juxtaposed against the selfishness
and animosity of the Pickles—and though he is endowed with wit
to lay bare arrogance and egotism, he also has compassion to aid the
virtuous. Exactly the same pattern is discernible in *Sir Launcelot
Greaves*, where the protagonist adopts the guise of a knight-errant
"to combat vice in all her forms, redress injuries, chastise oppression"; but though he pits himself against the insidious Ferret, the
Gobbles, Squire Sycamore, he also faces the perfect Aurelia Darnel,
honest Tom Clarke and Captain Crowe. In *Humphry Clinker* also,
as Jeremy points out, Bramble consistently encounters two kinds of
situations. In one his "blood rises at every instance of insolence and
cruelty, even where he himself is no way concerned; and ingratitude
makes his teeth chatter." But there is alternately a second kind of
situation, for "on the other hand, the recital of a generous, humane,
or grateful action, never fails to draw from him tears of approbation,
which he is often greatly distressed to conceal."
    Smollett's problem throughout the novels, however, is neither
metaphysical nor ideational. His concern is never in proving that
selfishness is "as universal, if not as natural" as benevolence—a task
which Ferguson, Adam Smith and a number of writers within the
Scottish School assume for themselves, in the attempt to harmonize

Mandeville and Shaftesbury. Only in *Sir Launcelot Greaves*, perhaps, does this thesis assume major proportions within Smollett. The antipodal nature of man represents for Smollett not an ethical problem which has to be deliberated, but rather a major assumption from which particular conflicts within the novels emanate. Thus, Smollett's concern is not with the theoretical reconciliation of ethical contraries, but rather with practical human conduct, with operational problems rising from a universe where both self-love and social-love are equally natural and equally pervasive.

How can man best operate within this kind of universe?—this is the problem confronting characters within the novels. Roderick Random, responding with indignation to selfishness, reveals a passion for benevolence; he must learn increasingly to reconcile these with reason and understanding if he is not to be taken in by appearances, and if he is to achieve his ultimate goals. Peregrine Pickle, who operates through wit and imagination, must learn to curb the fancy with judgment, if he is to succeed. Ferdinand Count Fathom falls short of his ends because of the excess of his arts and appetites, and eventually he must develop more spontaneity and warmth of heart. And Sir Launcelot Greaves must recognize the extravagance of his benevolence, if he is to survive in this temporal universe.

The reconciliation of passion with reason, imagination with judgment, nature with art, benevolence with self-love—these are the problems posed in Smollett's novels, with a culmination in the cultural relativity afforded by *Humphry Clinker*, in which ideas of primitivism are reconciled with ideas of progress.

Though for half a century after Smollett most novelists turned to doctrines and ideas in which characters were only thinking entities, the Scottish writer was never willing to subordinate the individual and his actions to the thoughts he himself held. Throughout Smollett, there is an insistence upon the organicism and congruity of man's inner life, an insistence which presupposes the individual as an acting whole, not as a stage on which concepts are assembled and reassembled. Like the Scottish group from which he sprang, the novelist rarely lost his wholeness, his common-sense approach, so basic to his craft. True, the plot in Smollett is sometimes thin and confusing, the situations frequently rambling and purposeless. But then the whole in Smollett is always perceptible and delightful, and offers consistent reason why this almost-forgotten writer should still vie with Fielding and Sterne for a major position in eighteenth-century English letters.

REFERENCES

1. George Morrow Kahrl, *Tobias Smollett, Traveler-Novelist* (Chicago, 1945). Louis L. Martz, *The Later Career of Tobias Smollett* (New Haven, 1942).

2. Alexander Carlyle, *Autobiography* (Edinburgh, 1860), p. 265. C. E. Jones, *Smollett Studies* (Berkeley, 1942), p. 75. *The Complete Works of William Hazlitt*, ed. P. P. Howe (London, 1931), VI, 115-17. See also *Monthly Magazine*, IV (1797), which comments that, like Fielding's, Smollett's novels are "subservient to the purposes of truth and philosophy." Compare this with Archibald Alison's assertion in *Essays Political, Historical, and Miscellaneous* (London, 1850), III, 322, that Smollett was neither "a poet nor a philosopher"; to search for philosophical views "was out of the question: it belonged neither to his age nor character to dream of anything of the kind." In a recent critical introduction to *Humphry Clinker* (New York, 1950), Robert Gorham Davis writes: "It is difficult to think of many writers of comparable stature who have been as little concerned as Smollett with the deeper ambiguities and conflicts of the human spirit, or have been less susceptible to the kind of symbolic, mythic, many-leveled interpretation which is central to modern criticism." Like Alison, Davis sees this lack of depth as a typical eighteenth-century quality, observing that Smollett had a "representatively eighteenth-century . . . mind, human-centered, common-sensical, and rationalistic."

3. Samuel T. Coleridge, *Works*, ed. W. C. T. Shedd (New York, 1853), IV, 277. James R. Foster, *History of the Pre-Romantic*

Novel in England (New York, 1949), pp. 120-30. Lewis M. Knapp, *Tobias Smollett* (Princeton, 1949), pp. 319-20. George Sherburn, *A Literary History of England*, ed. Albert C. Baugh *et al.* (New York, 1948), p. 962. *Monthly Chronicle*, I (1838), 50. See also Fred W. Boege, *Smollett's Reputation as a Novelist* (Princeton, 1947), p. 96, who attributes this ambiguity to shifting standards of taste, finding "Leigh Hunt (with the approval of Hazlitt) and Carlyle referring to scenes from Smollett as among the most pathetic in world literature," while later critics tend to "set down as one of the chief counts in their indictment of Smollett his brutality and lack of feeling for his characters."

4. *Critical Review*, XIII (1762), 427-29. Knapp, pp. 306-07. Foster, p. 125. Ernest M. Baker, *The History of the English Novel* (London, 1930), IV, 201-02.

5. Walter Scott, *Lives of Eminent Novelists and Dramatists* (London, n.d.), pp. 451-52. Carlyle, p. 191. *Critical Review*, VI (1758), 226-39. Letter to William Huggins, quoted in L. F. Powell, "William Huggins and Tobias Smollett," *MP*, XXXIV (1936), 185. Saintsbury's introduction to *Sir Launcelot Greaves* comments on "Smollett's Whiggery and Scotchmanship," whereas in the introduction to *Peregrine Pickle* we hear of "Smollett's Tory antipathy to ultra-Whigs." Davis, p. xv, observes that after writing his *History*, Smollett became "as a result, a Tory, because he found the Whig ministers such knaves." In Laurence Brander's *Tobias Smollett* (Colchester, 1951), p. 9, we learn also that "Smollett began with Whig leanings and only later on, as he worked, did he discover a Tory outlook." This is a position which Knapp, pp. 303-04, sustains. On the other hand, as acute a scholar as Thomas Seccombe, ed. *Works of Tobias Smollett* (Westminster, 1899-1901), XII, xiv, insists that "Smollett is clearly a political Ishmael, who has severed his ties with all parties."

6. Knapp, pp. 303-04.

7. Arthur O. Lovejoy, *The Great Chain of Being* (Cambridge, Mass., 1950). Ronald S. Crane, "English Criticism: Neo-Classical," in Joseph T. Shipley's *Dictionary of World Literature* (New York, 1943). Lois Whitney, *Primitivism and the Idea of Progress* (Baltimore, 1934). Walter Jackson Bate, *From Classic to Romantic* (Cambridge, Mass., 1946).

8. The most detailed reconstruction of Smollett's life is, of course, in the authoritative biography by Knapp, *op. cit.*

9. David Daiches offers an excellent analysis of the eighteenth-century Scottish tradition in his opening chapter of *Robert Burns* (New York, 1950). An excellent picture of the Scot in London during 1762-63 can be drawn from *Boswell's London Journal*, ed. Frederick A. Pottle (New Haven, Conn., 1950).

10. A. S. P. Woodhouse, "Romanticism and the History of Ideas," in *English Studies Today*, ed. C. L. Wrenn and G. Bullough (Oxford, 1951), pp. 120-40.

11. Compare Alfred North Whitehead's approach in *Science and the Modern World* (New York, 1926), pp. 199, 209, with that of Rudolf Metz, *A Hundred Years of British Philosophy* (New York, 1938), pp. 29 ff. Walter J. Hipple, Jr., "The Aesthetics of Dugald Stewart: Culmination of a Tradition," *JAAC*, XIV (1955), 77-96, is one of the few to consider the Scottish School relative to its own thought, rather than as a prolegomenon to Kant and the German idealists. Anthony Quinton in "The Neglect of Victorian Philosophy," *VS*, I (1958), 245-54, argues convincingly that an ignoral of the Scottish philosophers has done much in distorting the role played by the German idealists in English nineteenth-century thought.

12. Adam Ferguson, *An Essay on the History of Civil Society* (London, 1773), pp. 1-121.

13. Gladys Bryson, *Man and Society: The Scottish Inquiry of the Eighteenth Century* (Princeton, 1945), pp. 173-74. See also Harry Elmer Barnes and Howard Becker, *Social Thought from Lore to Science* (n.p., 1938), p. 545; W. C. Lehmann, *Adam Ferguson and the Beginnings of Modern Sociology* (New York, 1930), pp. 183 ff., 238 ff.

14. Roy Harvey Pearce, "The Eighteenth-Century Scottish Primitivists: Some Reconsiderations," *ELH*, XII (1945), 219-20.

15. Whitney, pp. 279 ff.

CHAPTER TWO. *RODERICK RANDOM:*

A Study in Reason and Passion

1. IN AN EARLY SECTION of *The Adventures of Roderick Random*, when the protagonist first arrives in London, he is enticed into gambling with several sharpers. Having already through rage and vanity lost all sense of discretion, he now proceeds to lose every shilling of his own money. A gentleman present sagely observes, "You are a young man, and your passions too impetuous; you must learn to govern them better" (I, 96). Before the close of the novel, Roderick has learned the wisdom of governing the passions and can announce that "the impetuous transports of my passion are now settled and mellowed" (III, 215-16).

Crucial to this decisive change which the hero effects between the beginning and ending of the novel is an ethical theme which provides the text with structure and meaning. Though this ethical theme is never as pervasive as in Johnson's *Rasselas*, or as tightly constructed as in Fielding's *Tom Jones*, its consistency warrants an examination of the text outside the picaresque tradition in which it has almost invariably been considered. Passionate, ebullient, a prey to his own untutored feelings as much as to the guile of a calloused world which artfully turns these feelings to its own advantage, Roderick must learn that only feelings controlled by reason, emotions reined by the understanding can be productive of the happiness and success he seeks.

The author's prefatory essay, which confesses that *Roderick Random* is modeled on Le Sage's plan for *Gil Blas*, is partially responsible for the frequent charge that Smollett is writing in the picaresque vein. In addition, Smollett's translation of *Gil Blas*, printed nine months after his own novel and reappearing in several editions during his lifetime, draws attention to the obvious parallels between the two texts. Despite manifest similarities between the episodic and adventurous development of Roderick Random and Gil Blas, subtle differences operating within Smollett's novel tend to ally it more with the moral tradition of eighteenth-century England than with the tradition of the *picaro*.

Smollett admits in his preface to modeling his novel on Le Sage's plan; but he also confesses that he has taken the liberty "to differ from him in the execution, where I thought his particular situations were uncommon, extravagant, or peculiar to the country in which the scene is laid." Whereas Le Sage aims to "excite mirth," Smollett intends to arouse "compassion" and "pity" for the protagonist, who must "engage the ingenuous more warmly in his behalf." Le Sage "deviates from probability" with sudden "transitions from distress to happiness," but Smollett proposes to avoid improbability which "prevents that generous indignation which ought to animate the reader against the sordid and vicious disposition of the world."

Because scholars who pursue the problem are invariably carried away by similitudes between the two authors, while ignoring *differentiae*, they fail to examine obvious implications of Smollett's proposal.[1] Clearly, his intentions are to shift from the picaresque manner; but a necessary corollary of belief in the "sordid and vicious" world is Smollett's aim to pit himself against the creed of the popular Shaftesburians who were posing a universe of harmony and goodness. Thus, the preface points to a centrality in *Roderick Random*, when the author declares his intention of revealing "the sordid and vicious disposition of the world" by thrusting Roderick into its midst, evoking sympathy for him, and thereby giving rise to "that generous indignation which ought to animate the reader" against the reality of selfishness and knavery.

Roderick's problem is to learn not only the nature of this world, but more important, how to act within a "sordid and vicious" universe. At first, his responses are dictated by his indignation, by feelings and passions, whose impetuousness consistently impedes the educational process. Eventually, he learns to bridle his passions with understanding, to govern the emotions with reason.

This conflict between reason and passion, internal to Roderick, and central to the development of the novel, is certainly one of the major problems with which eighteenth-century England was absorbed. In his *Essay on Human Understanding* Locke maintained that "Reason must be our last judge and guide in every thing" (IV, 19, 14), for "it penetrates into the depths of the sea and earth, elevates our thoughts as high as the stars, and leads us through the vast spaces, and large rooms of this mighty fabric" (IV, 17, 9). Though Swift is generally derisive of reason in its excess, he has Gulliver observe that the "noble Houyhnhnms are endowed by nature with a general disposition to all virtues, and have no conceptions or ideas of what is evil in a rational creature, so their grand maxim is to cultivate reason, and to be wholly governed by it." At the conclusion of his *Seventh Discourse* Sir Joshua Reynolds appears in perfect concurrence with Locke and Gulliver when he writes that the true artist must form his taste with reason and philosophy, which partake of the fixed, the permanent and the invariable. "In the midst of the highest flights of fancy or imagination, reason ought to preside from first to last. . . ." At the other extreme were men like Edward Young, who insisted in *Night Thoughts* that

> Humble Love
> And not proud Reason, keeps the door of Heav'n;
> Love finds admission, where proud Science fails;   (IX, 1856-58)

and that the passions, especially grief, have taught more "Than Genius, or proud Learning, e'er could boast" (V, 253-54). Terms of the controversy are apparent in Fielding's *Joseph Andrews*, where Lady Booby alternates between lust and discretion, until "the lady's passion got the better of her reason" (I, viii); in *The Man of Feeling*, where Henry Mackenzie describes Miss Walton—"her humanity was a feeling, not a principle" (XIII); and in *Vathek*, where William Beckford comments at the close upon the terrible fate of his sensuous protagonist: "Such was, and such should be, the punishment of unrestrained passions. . . ."

True, the term *reason* assumes variant connotations during the period. For some, particularly toward the early part of the century, it represents a faith in *a priori*, deductive, geometric principles; for others, and increasingly as the century progresses, it is a kind of "inner light" within the human heart, a comprehending faculty which enables men to grasp simple axiomatic truths. This shift in meaning is indicative of a major ideational conflict characteristic of the age, according to Hoxie N. Fairchild, whose examination of religious trends reveals a successive breakdown of rationalism into empiricism, then of empiricism into sentimentalism, with corresponding antagonisms that were at once religious, social, and political.[2] These same antagonisms have also been perceived in eighteenth-century attitudes toward nature. As the century progressed, man's "nature" was to be found not in his "reason," but rather in his emotions, his instincts, and his sensibilities, Basil Willey writes. With the growth of sensibility, Rousseau's *je sens, donc je suis* gradually displaced the Cartesian *cogito, ergo sum*.[3] In the same light, Lois Whitney's study of primitivism reveals "a transition during the century from a rationalistic primitivism at the beginning, which tended to derive the qualities of goodness and sagacity in the savage from the unobstructed operation of the 'light of reason.' " Eventually, she concludes, "a more emotional, sentimental, and antinomian primitivism . . . became increasingly the favored type as the century progressed."[4] This same conflict—observed in religion, in concepts of nature, in ideas of primitivism— has been equally detected in the epistemology of morals, for the question whether moral choice is the result of knowing or of feeling became an important distinction among the eighteenth-century moralists.[5]

Though *reason* and *passion* were terms inherently antithetical for most of the century, there were some who found them related and complementary. Thus, Pope writes in the *Essay on Man* that "On life's vast ocean diversely we sail, / Reason the card, but Passion is the gale" (II, 107-08); and observes that "Reason, Passion, answer one great aim" (IV, 395). From a different perspective, Goldsmith in *The Vicar of Wakefield* has Mr. Burchell insist:

> I have ever perceived, that where the mind was capacious, the affections were good. And indeed Providence seems kindly our friend in this particular, thus to debilitate the understanding where the heart is corrupt, and diminish the power where there is the will to do mischief. (XV)

This interrelation between head and heart, reason and feeling, is at work also in Mackenzie's *Man of Feeling*. Here both sympathy and satire are evoked for the protagonist—sympathy for Harley's sensibilities, and satire for their excess—just as they are evoked by Goldsmith for his vicar, whose lack of understanding can be gently satirized, without deprecating the innate goodness of his benevolent passions. The impassioned Harley agrees that "the world, in the eye of a philosopher, may be said to be a large madhouse" and asserts that "the passions of men are temporary madnesses; and sometimes very fatal in their effects" (XX). But these are not contradictions of his own tenets, for he is attempting to define those limits of sentiment, beyond which reason must supply a guiding force.

Most of these reconciliations are certainly developed with precision by the writers who had their roots in Scotland during the eighteenth century. In his *Essay on the History of Civil Society* Adam Ferguson asserts the mediating position of the group, observing that especially in social actions "the understanding appears to borrow very much from the passions; and there is a felicity of conduct in human affairs, in which it is difficult to distinguish the promptitude of the head from the ardour and sensibility of the heart." Where these are united, among primitive cultures or among civilized societies, is to be discerned true superiority. Hence, we judge men, not on the basis of what they know or how they feel, but in what they do or how they perform.[6]

With a view closely aligned with that of Ferguson, George Turnbull explains in *Observations upon Liberal Education* that "it is reason's business to compute and ballance pleasures and pains of all kinds," to become "well-educated, or formed into a really useful, because into a governing principle." Only then can man master himself:

> This disposition is what is properly called virtue or strength of mind: Without it one must be feeble and unsteady, unable to act firmly and regularly a reasonable or becoming part in life: Nay, he must be the sport of contradictory passions and appetites. It is by it alone that one can attain to that harmony and consistency of affections and manners which create peace within, and command, trust, love and reverence from all around.

Apropos the dichotomous views prevalent among his contemporaries, Turnbull counsels that youth ought to be taught early

> to take a just view of human nature, and to consider man as he really is, neither as a merely sensitive being, nor as a merely intellectual or moral one, but as a compound. . . . For in the human composition, those two different sorts of powers and affections are so intimately blended, that it is impossible to avoid errors . . . if one class of them be considered separately and independently of the other.[7]

This same concept, central to Turnbull's educational views and Ferguson's socio-historical perspective, is pervasive in Hugh Blair's esthetic in *Lectures on Rhetoric*. For Blair, taste is "a sort of compound power, in which the light of understanding always mingles, more or less, with the feelings of sentiment." Though taste is "founded on a certain natural and instinctive sensibility to beauty, yet reason . . . assists taste in many of its operations, and serves to enlarge its power," Blair writes, for "as a sound head, so likewise

a good heart, is a very material requisite to just taste." Founded on
sensibility and developed by reason, taste manifests in its most improved state two characteristics, delicacy and correctness. These
"mutually imply each other," though "Delicacy leans more to feeling; correctness, more to reason and judgment." The former is a
gift of nature, the latter, of art. Blair's aim, seemingly, is to refute
the conflicting schools, the one attributing good taste wholly to
reason, the other attributing it wholly to feeling:

> The difference between the authors who found the standard of taste
> upon the common feelings of human nature ascertained by general
> approbation, and those who found it upon established principles
> which can be ascertained by reason, is more an apparent than a real
> difference. . . . These two systems . . . differ in reality very little
> from one another. Sentiment and reason enter into both; and by
> allowing to each of these powers its due place, both systems may be
> rendered consistent. Accordingly, it is in this light that I have
> endeavoured to place the subject.[8]

In *The Theory of Moral Sentiments* Adam Smith offers a view
typical of the Scottish Common-Sense group, with its reconciliation
of passions and reason. With acknowledgment to Francis Hutcheson, who "had the merit of being the first who distinguished, with
any degree of precision, in what respect all moral distinctions may
be said to arise from reason, and in what respect they are founded
upon immediate sense and feeling," Smith pointedly relates moral
judgment to pleasure and pain:

> Pleasure and pain are the great objects of desire and aversion; but
> these are distinguished not by reason but by immediate sense and
> feeling. If virtue, therefore, be desirable for its own sake, and if vice
> be in the same manner the object of aversion, it cannot be reason
> which originally distinguishes those different qualities, but imme-
> diate sense and feeling.

Reason, on the other hand, "cannot render any particular object
either agreeable or disagreeable to the mind for its own sake." It can

only show "that this object is the means of obtaining some other which is naturally either pleasing or displeasing, and in this manner may render it either agreeable or disagreeable, for the sake of something else." First perceptions, then, are always of immediate sense and feeling, whereas the function of reason is to discover general rules of justice by which we can regulate our actions and determine what is prudent, decent, generous, or noble. According to Smith, then, virtue consists of reason which is arrived at through experience and induction, with approbation and disapprobation operating as regulating forces for desires and aversions, though also arrived at from our perception of pleasure and pain.[9]

Apparent in any examination of the Scottish group, regardless of the writer's perspective, is that *reason* is neither the deductive, *a priori*, geometric principle of the early rationalists, nor wholly the "inner light" of the later moralists. Rather, it is a practical, common-sense mode of behavior, which does not deny the efficacy or validity of the emotional life, but simply regulates and governs the feelings, directing them toward some ethical and/or esthetic goal. Thomas Reid defines this middle ground as a branch of reason, for which two functions can be ascribed:

> The first is to judge of things self-evident; the second to draw conclusions that are not self-evident from those that are. The first of these is the province, and the sole province, of common sense; and, therefore, it coincides with reason in its whole extent, and is only another name for one branch or one degree of reason.

Thus, "a man of sense is a man of judgment. Good sense is good judgment," Reid writes. "Common sense is that degree of judgment which is common to men with whom we can converse and transact business."[10]

"Good sense," as Reid defines it, approaches with close approximation the goal Smollett formulates in *Roderick Random*, where the protagonist faces the "sordid and vicious disposition of the world." If we assume that *reason* and *passion* are terms inherently antithetical for the century, then Smollett's novel appears formless and contradictory.[11] On the other hand, if we grant Smollett his own assumptions, those gleaned perceptively from the Scottish School, then much in *Roderick Random* assumes a form and meaning which have hitherto eluded critics.

2. RODERICK RANDOM is certainly no pallid imitation of Gil Blas; nor, set against the tradition of rogue literature, is he even consistently the *pícaro*, for he makes his way in the world with moral pride and righteous indignation—not with the ingenuity and cunning, cruel hoaxes and acquisitiveness, usually viewed as the essence of the picaresque hero. Only twice an apprentice, once a servant, rarely a rogue, never a witty swindler, Roderick is hardly the anti-hero whom we might identify with Lazarillo de Tormes or Jonathan Wild.

Roderick is primarily a man of strong and impetuous passions. Expressed throughout the novel in fiery, burning images, these passions erupt with frequency and violence at the slightest provocation. The fiery disposition is symbolized best, perhaps, by his deep red hair. Although the flaming locks are shorn soon after his arrival in London, there is hardly a corresponding shift in character. Strap tells him, "You was always fiery" (I, 130), and Roderick is himself cognizant of a "disposition, which was touchy and impatient of control" (III, 8), of "passions, at any time high" (I, 139). Even as a boy, he bears a "disposition, impatient of affronts" (I, 8). In London he is chided for possessing "passions too impetuous" (I, 96). Unjustly charged by his apothecary master, Mr. Lavement, with stealing supplies, he is "fired with . . . resentment and disdain" (I, 152). The malice of Crampley, lieutenant aboard the *Lizzard*, adds "fuel" to his resentment, and though Roderick stifles the "flame" (I, 120), we discover that "indignation, which had boiled so long within," erupts once they step on dry land. In a "transport of fury" and "rage" Roderick hurls himself at his antagonist, though he is overcome and abandoned upon the beach, until his "passion insensibly abated" (II, 127-28). Fleeced by an unscrupulous capuchin, he is "boiling with indignation" and "so much transported with grief, anger, and disdain, that a torrent of blood gushed from my nostrils" (II, 171-72).

Erupting at the slightest provocation, these passions express themselves in two extremes. There is anger or indignation at the tyranny of a schoolmaster; at barbarous insults from his fellow students; at the unscrupulous artfulness of gamblers; at the injustice of the apothecary, Lavement; at the malice and abuse of Crampley; or at the deception of the capuchin. But there is also the warmth or generosity with which Roderick responds to benevolence or distress.

His affection for Strap is an example of this more generous passion—although critics who approach him with standards more Victorian than eighteenth-century have distorted the relationship to Roderick's disadvantage. Sir Walter Scott, recognizing problems of social stratification in this novel, has commented that "in Scotland, at that period, the absolute devotion of a follower to his master was something which entered into, and made part of the character of the lower ranks in general; and therefore domestic fidelity was regarded as a thing more of course than in England."[12] Smollett obviously assumes this kind of social milieu within the novel, for he notes that "there is no part of the world in which the peasants are more attached to their lords than in Scotland" (III, 213). The reciprocal affection of Strap and Roderick, then, need never imply a disintegration of rank. Roderick is told by Strap "it was more reasonable and decent that he [Strap] should depend upon me [Roderick] who was a gentleman, than that I should be controlled by him" (I, 99).[13] Indeed, Roderick's indignation stems in part from this belief in social degree, since he "laid claim to the character of a gentleman, by birth, education, and behaviour" (III, 88), a role which society has denied him almost from the beginning. Although his behavior to Strap may appear ungenerous, he is simply operating within a given social framework which demands a lessening of intimacy once Roderick achieves some kind of rank. Mainly, his relationship with Strap is indicative of the benevolent passions at work. His early meeting with Strap, employed as barber in Newcastle, occasions a "transport of . . . joy" and "mutual caresses" (I, 42-43). In London, relieved by Strap's offer of his entire purse, he finds himself "so touched with the generous passion of this poor creature, that I could not refrain from weeping" (I, 98). In prison, Roderick begs permission for Strap to sit at the same table with him, despite their difference in rank (III, 137).

Roderick's generous passions are not restricted to Strap's person. The lamentable condition of Miss Williams, the diseased prostitute, fills Roderick "with sympathy and compassion" (II, 29), for admittedly, his is a heart "naturally prone to every tender passion" (I, 157). In Jamaica, reunited with the tender-hearted Thomson, whom he has long given up for dead, Roderick is overcome with a torrent of emotion: "It was some time ere I recovered the use of my reason, overpowered with this event, and longer still before I could speak; so that all I was capable of was to return his embraces, and to mingle the overflowings of my joy with his" (II, 116). In his first reunion with his beloved Narcissa, he finds himself "elevated by my passion above every other consideration," and abandons himself to his inner feelings:

> Good Heaven! what were the thrillings of my soul at that instant! my reflection was overwhelmed with a torrent of agitation! my heart throbbed with surprising violence! a sudden mist overspread my eyes! my ears were invaded with a dreadful sound! I paused for want of breath, and, in short, was for some moments entranced!

So strong are these emotions that his "faculties were overborne by the tide" and his "soul was agonised with rapture" at this "passion for the loveliest of your sex—a passion which took possession of my soul." His "senses were lost in ecstasy," and he "grew mad with admiration" (III, 81-93).[14]

These two extremes in Roderick Random, the affection and the hostility, the joyous love and the bitter antagonism, are clearly

indicative of the dual world with which the protagonist is confronted—a universe which is Hobbesian, as well as Shaftesburian.
But more particularly, these are indicative of the dichotomy inherent in Roderick himself, whose uncontrollable passions leave him
with a temperament that is divided into opposing halves and incapable of facing the problems of a morally bifurcated world. Victim
of a behavioristic pattern that is frequently self-destructive and
therefore incapable of achieving goals, Roderick persistently suffers
from his own lack of understanding. True, his passions—the indignation as well as the affection—act as major sustaining forces, aid-
ing the protagonist in his search for happiness; for, as he himself
notes, "It was happy for me that I had a good deal of resentment in
my constitution, which animated me on such occasions against the
villany of mankind, and enabled me to bear misfortunes otherwise
intolerable" (II, 171). But these passions serve also as impediments
which actively prevent, by their very excess, any basic fulfillment.

As a consequence, Roderick often proves a victim to his own
indiscretion. Although in boyhood his passionate disposition enables him to be "inured to adversity," at the same time, as he himself later recognizes, it "involved me in a thousand troublesome
adventures" (I, 8). The apothecary, Mr. Lavement, reminds him:
" 'Ah! mon pauvre Roderique! you ave more of de véracité dan of de
prudence' " (I, 150). The youth's animosity to Potion's "mean
selfish disposition" is expressed with an "indignation which . . .
gave me spirits to support my reverse of fortune"; but simultaneously, since the passion reveals more virtue than discretion, Potion's
suggestion that he remain in his present lodging for another week is
rejected, and Roderick sallies out "in a transport of rage and sorrow,
without knowing whither to fly for shelter, having not one friend in
the world capable of relieving me, and only three shillings in my
purse." Still boiling with indignation, he approaches a seeming
friend for advice and assistance, only to recognize too late that "this
heat of mine gave him all the advantage he desired over me, and
our discourse, after much altercation, concluded in his desiring
never to see me again" (I, 31-32). When Squire Gawky proves un-

sympathetic, malicious, and cowardly, Roderick, though it costs him his gold-laced hat to defray expenses, indignantly has the story inserted in the news, from "the desire of revenge." Here, too, his passion for justice over-rides all circumspection, for "the fumes of my resentment being dissipated, as well as the vanity of my success, I found myself deserted to all the horrors of extreme want, and avoided by mankind as a creature of a different species" (I, 33-34). Aboard *H. M. S. Thunder*, where he is addressed with some insolence by an officer, Roderick "foolishly answered, with a countenance that too plainly declared the state of my thoughts." Again veracity exceeds prudence, and as a result, he is damned for a saucy son of a bitch, lashed, and flung into irons (II, 36).

Roderick's lack of discretion, his inability to discipline his passions through reason, is only part of his larger defect: a signal lack of understanding, of both self and the external world. To be sure, Roderick, as narrator, frequently acknowledges an understanding of society's "selfishness and roguery" (II, 161), and is quick to assert "the villany of mankind" (II, 171), its "knavery and selfishness" (III, 162). But usually these insights are the posterior reconstruction of an ethical complex by the narrator in his function as memoir-writer, and not necessarily a facet of Roderick's understanding during his youth. Statements of self-insight scattered throughout the novel must therefore be approached with caution. It is essential to distinguish between the two roles which Random assumes throughout: as the mature, reflective writer of memoirs looking back in time, and as the young, impassioned adventurer looking forward in anticipation. Though we learn of Roderick that "pride and resentment . . . were two chief ingredients in my disposition" (I, 135), or that "pride and resentment had rendered [him] utterly incapable of the least submission to [inhumaneness]" (II, 114), these again are more the later insights of the reflective narrator than the self-knowledge of the young protagonist. This double role itself indicates an important change occurring between the rash youth at the opening and the rational maturity encountered at the close of the novel. Also, it reinforces the necessity for not assuming any major degree of understanding for the youth Roderick, when his impassioned behavior belies the presence of rational contemplation.

Roderick's actions throughout the early sections of the novel are more than indicative of this consistent defect in the understanding. Like Renaldo, who in *Ferdinand Count Fathom* is easily beguiled because his own generous feelings frequently confuse appearances of benevolence with a reality of egotism, Random frequently mistakes the selfish Hobbesian for the humane Shaftesburian. When in an impoverished state the protagonist approaches his friend for aid, he finds him at first "wonderfully affected with the misery of my condition, and looked upon him as a man of the most extensive sympathy and benevolence" (I, 31); but he is not left under this misapprehension for long. Again, en route with Strap to London, they lodge at a public house, where "the landlord . . . seemed to be a venerable old man," who "gave Strap such an idea of his benevolence, that he positively believed we should pay nothing for our lodging and entertainment." Roderick admits that he "was partly of Strap's opinion"; and both share disillusionment the following morning, when they are presented with an unconscionable bill (I, 59 ff.). In London he learns early that a gentleman whom he has looked upon as a "polite, honest, friendly, humane person . . . was no other than a rascally money-dropper, who made it his business to decoy strangers" (I, 99); he is beguiled by Cringer and Staytape, taken in by Beau Jackson, and almost marries a whore who appears to be a wealthy heiress.

Not until he learns more of the world and the self does Roderick succeed in achieving the position and affluence which he pursues relentlessly throughout the novel. As Smollett points out in his preface, his hero must face and conquer two opposing forces, the self-love of mankind and the inexperience of self:

> I have attempted to represent modest merit struggling with every difficulty to which a friendless orphan is exposed, from his own want of experience, as well as from the selfishness, envy, malice, and base indifference of mankind.

A heightened understanding and a reasoned discipline of emotions must for Roderick precede any achievement of goals. The twin horses of indignation and compassion, which throughout early sections of the novel succeed with little effort in pulling him at random, at their own whim and fancy, must be reined and governed; the whole world must become an academy, with reason the bridling force.

3. IN STRUCTURE, as well as characterization, *Roderick Random* has been identified with the picaresque tradition. Sir Walter Scott, who has been frequently paraphrased, found the adventures "forming no connected plot or story, the several parts of which hold connexion with, or bear proportion to, each other." Almost inevitably, plot is described as amorphous and episodic, with the various adventures disconnected except through their relationship to the central character.[15]

Those critics who have followed Scott's views are not without some validity. A superficial glance at organization can perhaps divide the novel into six distinct parts, each containing its own geographic locale and a particular social stratum in which Roderick operates; each part in turn containing a series of smaller adventures, provided with their own catastrophes, from which the protagonist is inevitably rescued by a kind of *deus ex machina*.

The First Part (I-VII), staged in Scotland and centering about Roderick's youth and education, opens with the injustice and hardships Roderick encounters with his grandfather, his cousins, his schoolmaster. From these he is almost immediately rescued by the intercession of a nautical Pallas Athena, his uncle Tom Bowling. Before the close of this section, the benevolent god Bowling, himself the victim of higher Olympian laws, is forced to withdraw his generous support, and young Rory is thrown upon his own resources.

The Second Part (VIII-XXIII), centered about London, finds Rory aided somewhat by his own wits, though also by his friend Strap and the prostitute Miss Williams, neither of whom of course is a god. Therefore, after a brief career as journeyman apothecary, he is left destitute for a second time.

At the beginning of the Third Part (XXIV-XXXVII) some lesser and malignant divinities, substituting one misfortune for another, press him aboard the *Thunder*, a man-of-war. Nevertheless, he succeeds in rising to the position of surgeon's mate—through his own abilities, but also through the aid of Thomson and Morgan. A fight with Captain Crampley, once the ship founders, results in his being wounded, robbed, and left destitute for a third time. When no one else will aid him, a minor goddess, Mrs. Sagely, takes him in, heals his wounds, and provides him with a position in Sussex. Here, during the Fourth Part (XXVIII-XLI), he serves as domestic to Narcissa and her aunt.

Removed to France in the Fifth Part (XLII-LXIII) by some evil water sprites, a band of smugglers, he is rescued from an ignominious fate as an impoverished soldier by the divine intercession of Strap. Now a wealthy gentleman, Strap can offer the generous aid necessary for Roderick's return to London. Once more in England, Rory tries his hand at fortune-hunting. When this fails, he strives to arrange for a political sinecure. After this also fails, he determines to pursue only the heart of his "divine Narcissa." Again, he endures a series of misfortunes, is impoverished and jailed.

In the Sixth Part (LXIV-LXIX), once more rescued by the great god Bowling, he is induced to leave on a series of voyages as ship's surgeon, during which he encounters a long-lost father, now wealthy, and can therefore return to England and marry Narcissa.

Admittedly, this is only a superficial examination of the picaresque plot in its barest outline. Immediately perceptible is a medley of adventures, relying heavily upon the use of surprise and the unexpected, and connected by the character of the protagonist as much as by the rapidity of motion and gusto which the narrator brings to the multiplicity of incidents. This is typical of *Gil Blas*, the model picaresque tale for the eighteenth century, just as it is typical of the whole tradition of rogue literature emerging from Spain in the mid-sixteenth century after the publication of *Lazarillo de Tormes*. But these devices are also part of the stock-in-trade of Elizabethan dramatists, who inherited them from the Roman comic writers.

Any dismissal of plot in *Roderick Random* as typically picaresque, however, necessarily fails to account for a number of significant factors. For one, there is Smollett's moral intent, as revealed in the prefatory essay. Second, there is the obvious problem, internal to Roderick and crucial to the development of his character, the conflict between the passions and the understanding. Third, minor characters are assigned roles in Roderick's struggle, ostensibly to reinforce Smollett's moral intent. Next, the change Roderick undergoes by the close of the novel, the modification of his passions, is neither totally unexpected nor completely surprising, for it has been prepared for, though crudely and with an unwieldiness that modern critics, with their emphasis upon a tight construction, might find untenable. Further, the final series of adventures which move the hero away from his immediate goals, against his better judgment, take on meaning relative only to the ethical theme, for it would have been possible to restore Roderick to society through the offices of Tom Bowling with position and sufficient wealth to marry Narcissa and achieve the happy ending essential to the comic romance. Finally, the tales of Mrs. Sagely, Tom Bowling, Thomson, Captain Oregan, and Don Rodrigo—which in a picaresque novel would have assumed the length of an episode or *historiette*—have all, for some reason, been minimized and obviously foreshortened to keep the major narrative running.

If we move outside the picaresque tradition and try to examine *Roderick Random* as a forerunner of the "novel of learning" exemplified by Goethe's *Wilhelm Meister,* then much is irrelevant to the organic growth of Smollett's protagonist and certainly cannot be accounted for. Many of Roderick's adventures are indubitably

self-sufficient, cumulative rather than progressive, and their se-
quence could be transposed almost at random. Indeed, the protagonist's name is itself indicative of the haphazard and random
way in which he lives, without the guidance of a governing mind.
As long as the passions hold sway, the adventures must necessarily
be experienced in a desultory fashion, more or less at the mercy of
chance.

Roderick Random is neither wholly picaresque nor wholly a
novel of learning; but, partaking of both, it achieves its own form.
This is a form dictated partially by the very nature of the protagonist
and the problem he faces—though Smollett's inexperience with the
genre at this early date certainly contributes to the random structure.

Granted its own inherent form, crude and unwieldly as it may
be, Roderick Random falls into two perceptible parts. The first section (I-LXIII), comprising a series of adventures with Random at
the mercy of his unbridled passions, plunges the protagonist into
the lowest depths. The second section (LXIV-LXIX) reveals the
triumph of reason which, coupled with the passions, now enables
him to control his own destiny and to achieve those goals which he
has set for himself.

Five distinct catastrophes, each greater than the last, are contained within the first section, as the protagonist learns increasingly
the disparity between his ends and his means, between the happiness and orderly existence he desires, and the pride and passionate
ebullience he consistently uses to achieve these ends.

His first "reverse of fortune" (I, 31-34), when Tom Bowling
is forced to withdraw his generous support of Roderick's education,
arouses in him an impassioned rage. Moved to revenge against his
false friends, Roderick finds himself almost immediately "deserted
to all the horrors of extreme want, and avoided by mankind as a
creature of a different species, or rather as a solitary being, no ways
comprehended within the scheme or protection of Providence. My
despair had rendered me almost quite stupefied."

A second catastrophe (I, 155), following his discharge as a
thief from Mr. Lavement's services, has more severe consequences:

> I found myself, by the iniquity of mankind, in a much more de-
> plorable condition than ever: for though I had been formerly as
> poor, my reputation was without blemish, and my health unim-
> paired till now; but at present my good name was lost, my money
> gone, my friends were alienated, my body was infected by a distemper
> contracted in the course of an amour, and my faithful Strap, who
> alone could yield me pity and assistance, absent I knew not where.

A third catastrophe (II, 127-28), following a long and arduous
rise in the navy and culminating in his furious attack on the malicious Crampley, reveals Roderick's passions at their highest pitch.
Now, he is alone, impoverished, severely wounded, completely
stripped of possessions, and left for dead on a strange shore.

> In this deplorable situation, exposed to the rage of an incensed bar-
> barian, and the rapine of an inhuman crew, I remained for some time;
> . . . when I recovered the use of understanding, I found myself
> alone in a desolate place, stripped of my clothes, money, watch,
> buckles, and everything but my shoes, stockings, breeches, and shirt.
> What a discovery must this have been to me, who but an hour before
> was worth sixty guineas in cash! I cursed the hour of my birth, the
> parents that gave me being, the sea that did not swallow me up, the
> poignard of the enemy, which could not find the way to my heart,
> the villany of those who had left me in that miserable condition; and
> in the ecstasy of despair, resolved to lie still where I was, and perish.

His fourth reversal (II, 172), after a brief respite with Narcissa and her aunt, takes place in France, where he is isolated on
alien soil, and abandoned like an animal to famine:

> My rage forsook me; I began to feel the importunate cravings of
> nature, and relapsed into silent sorrow, and melancholy reflection.
> I resolved all the crimes I had been guilty of, and found them so few
> and venial, that I could not comprehend the justice of that Provi-
> dence, which, after having exposed me to so much wretchedness and
> danger, left me a prey to famine at last in a foreign country, where I
> had not one friend or acquaintance to close my eyes, and do the last
> offices of humanity to my miserable carcase. A thousand times I
> wished myself a bear, that I might retreat to woods and deserts, far

from the hospitable haunts of man, where I could live by my own talents, independent of treacherous friends, and supercilious scorn.

Here, for the first time, the rage and impassioned indignation are displaced by somber contemplation; the excessive feelings give way before "melancholy reflection." He is moved, not so much by an emotional condemnation of mankind as by his own rational desire to "comprehend the justice of . . . Providence." Though he wishes himself a bear, he is obviously cognizant of the social distinction between rational man and the passionate brute, which does not allow him to retreat from society and live by his own talents.

His fifth reversal (III, 162-63), once he is arrested for debts and imprisoned in the Marshalsea, reduces him to the lowest depths to which his unbridled passions have taken him. Physically and morally disintegrated, in a prison from which there is no perceptible relief, he abandons himself to a complete acceptance of his lot:

> I . . . grew negligent of life, lost all appetite, and degenerated into such a sloven, that during the space of two months, I was neither washed, shifted, nor shaved; so that my face, rendered meagre with abstinence, was obscured with dirt, and overshadowed with hair, and my whole appearance squalid and even frightful.

This time his indignation is not at the injustice he himself endures, but at the greater abuse suffered by another, Melopoyn, the prisoner with nothing on him but an old rug. If he does not give way to absolute sorrow or despair, it is only because he is aware, for perhaps the first time, of the real dual nature of society, which encompasses not only a "perfidious world," but also "the amiable Narcissa."

> Notwithstanding all I had suffered from the knavery and selfishness of mankind, I was amazed and incensed at the base indifference which suffered such uncommon merit as he possessed to languish in obscurity, and struggle with all the miseries of a loathsome jail; and should have blessed the occasion that secluded me from such a perfidious world, had not the remembrance of the amiable Narcissa preserved my attachment to that society of which she constituted a part.

The five reversals seem to indicate that these crises are not wholly arbitrary, although the adventures preceding them may be, for they move with a pattern scarcely fortuitous toward the culmination afforded in the final section of the novel. The protagonist tries harder and harder to achieve the happiness and orderly existence of which he thinks himself deserving; but because of his consistent lack of understanding, he manages to fall lower and lower with each successive attempt. Only after this fifth and final catastrophe, when Tom Bowling rescues him from the prison, does he succeed in rescuing himself from the prison constructed by his own unruly passions.

4. THE DEVELOPMENT implicit in the five catastrophes is not the only preparation Smollett affords for Roderick's final reversal of situation and character, which reconciles passion with reason. In a limited sense, the protagonist has been aware throughout the novel of his excesses and has attempted to moderate them within his capabilities.

As early as his first reversal, having been dismissed from Potion's lodgings, and finding himself apprenticed to Launcelot Crab, he resolves to "study Crab's temper with all the application, and manage it with all the address, in my power." By developing his own understanding, Roderick achieves an "ascendency over him [Crab] in a short time, and . . . fortune began to wear a kinder aspect." Before long, even Squire Gawky, who has reason to fear Roderick's indignation, returns to town "without running any risk from my resentment, which was by this time pretty much cooled, and restrained by prudential reasons" (I, 37-39). Consequently, Roderick experiences his first internal change, as he turns to reason —neither *a priori*, geometric principles, nor an "inner light," but practical, common-sense learning, gleaned from experience—for his *modus vivendi*:

> I was no longer a pert unthinking coxcomb, giddy with popular applause, and elevated with the extravagance of hope: my misfortunes

had taught me how little the caresses of the world, during a man's
prosperity, are to be valued by him; and how seriously and expedi-
tiously he ought to set about making himself independent of them.
My present appearance, therefore, was the least of my care, which
was wholly engrossed in laying up a stock of instruction that might
secure me against the caprice of fortune for the future. (I, 38-39)

Again, with Mr. Lavement he pretends ignorance of French,
that he "might possible discover something in discourse, which
would either yield me amusement or advantage" (I, 132); and as
a result of this astuteness, "my life became much more agreeable
. . . and, as I every day improved in my knowledge of the town,
I shook off my awkward air by degrees" (I, 141). Similarly, though
his passions demand revenge against his old enemy Crampley, common sense leaves him "resolved to wait for a more convenient opportunity" (II, 120-21). In his first reunion with Tom Bowling,
whose benevolence he has always ascribed "to the dictates of a heart
as yet undebauched by a commerce with mankind" (I, 26), Roderick already has sufficient understanding to realize that his own
situation is less miserable than Bowling's, "because I was better
acquainted with the selfishness and roguery of mankind, consequently less liable to disappointment and imposition" (II, 161).
Although his knowledge steadily improves, he is not without
occasional errors in judgment. Having been beguiled by Beau Jackson, he is too quickly on his guard against the benevolent Thomson,
"fully resolved . . . not to be deceived by him so much to my
prejudice as I had been by the beau" (I, 106). He is taken in by
the capuchin, Frère Balthazar, who mistakenly "seemed to be of a
complexion too careless and sanguine to give me any apprehension"
(II, 169). He knows enough of the world to avoid commerce with
a seemingly wealthy courtesan (II, 191) and to save Strap from a
matrimonial trap with a tallow-chandler's widow who reveals "a
particular prominence of belly" attributed to a difficulty with her
liver (III, 1). Still, he is quite the novice with the arts of Melinda
and the "paternal caresses" of Lord Strutwell. He recognizes the
excesses of Narcissa's aunt, who is "too much of a philosopher to

be swayed by the customs of the world, . . . and therefore is frequently so absent, as to commit very strange mistakes and extravagances" (II, 136). He sees through Frère Balthazar, who, while professing the contemplative life, "loved good eating and drinking better than his rosary, and paid more adoration to a pretty girl than to the Virgin Mary, or St. Geneviève" (II, 167). And he is guarded against the theological excesses of the Scottish priest who urges him "to be persuaded by reason," so that "the grosser appetites [might be] subdued and chastised, and the soul wafted to divine regions of philosophy and truth, on the wings of studious contemplation" (II, 166). However, he fails to perceive the slightest parallel between Miss Williams' tale and his own life, and to learn from her experience the necessity for curbing his passions. Like him, she has refined sentiments, having been encouraged to read the moral extremists, "Shaftesbury, Tindal, Hobbes, and all the books that are remarkable for their deviation from the old way of thinking"; but like Roderick also, she fails to develop judgment, and therefore curses her "education, that, by refining my sentiments, made my heart the more susceptible." Like him, she sinks lower and lower in society, as she "obey[s] the dictates of rage, insolence, and lust" (II, 2-19). In comparing their situations, Roderick finds hers the more wretched. Yet he fails to perceive the moral to which her tale obviously points—the depths to which his own rage and insolence will lead him, if they continue unabated.

Not until the final section of the novel does the force of his experiences succeed in turning him aside from passion to reason, as he determines to concentrate upon the virtues of "the amiable Narcissa" rather than to vent his spleen upon the "perfidious world."

This decision to emphasize the positive virtues rather than the negative, the affectionate passions rather than the hostile, necessarily involves a change in manner, as well as in ends. Although Bowling offers him a "method of getting a fortune" once he is removed from prison, Roderick recognizes now, and for the first time, that wealth is an inferior pursuit, and that Bowling's is "a proposal that offered violence to my love." Ultimately he agrees to

Bowling's proposition, but only because of his affection for and obligation to his generous uncle, and not because of indignant claims to affluence and fortune to which he thinks himself "entitled by birth and education," and which have been denied him by a "perfidious world." Common sense turns him toward his new goals; and common sense allows him to pursue the wealth and position which only passionate indignation has sought before. With this belated recognition Roderick faces upon his release from prison a "sudden transition, which affected me more than any reverse I had formerly felt; and a crowd of incoherent ideas rushed so impetuously upon my imagination, that my reason could neither separate nor connect them" (III, 165-67).

It is his reason that Roderick appeals to, when he convinces Narcissa of the necessity he was under "to leave her, [and] reconcile[s] her to that event, by describing the advantages that in all probability would attend it" (III, 172). It is his reason that Mrs. Sagely successfully addresses, when he is torn by grief and doubt at the thought of parting from Narcissa, for she "opposed the tumults of my grief with such strength of reason, that my mind regained in some measure its tranquillity" (III, 176). It is his recently gained reason that Don Rodrigo, his new-found father, points to, when he perceives that his son's adversity has been in some measure a good, for it has "enlarged the understanding, improved the heart, steeled the constitution, and qualified a young man for all the duties and enjoyments of life, much better than any education which affluence could bestow" (III, 188). During Roderick's final reunion with Narcissa, he finds once more that his "passion grew turbulent and unruly . . . giddy with standing on the brink of bliss." Now, however, he possesses a governing power—"my virtue and philosophy." This power is admittedly "scarce sufficient to restrain the inordinate sallies of desire"; but Narcissa, who "perceived the conflict within" of passion and philosophy, succeeds in restraining him and reconciling the conflict with "her usual dignity of prudence" (III, 202). Eventually, the narrator himself discloses in the final paragraphs of the novel that indignation has vanished and affection holds sway: "If there be such a thing as true happiness on earth I enjoy it. The impetuous transports of my passion are now settled and mellowed into endearing fondness and tranquillity of love" (III, 215-16).

The stages through which young Roderick develops are paralleled most closely in *Elements of Moral Philosophy*, where David Fordyce, like Smollett, assumes that man is properly a compound of two states:

> The Passions are mere Force or Power, blind Impulses, acting violently and without Choice, and ultimately tending each to their respective Objects, without Regard to the Interest of the others, or of the whole System. Whereas the Directing and Judging Powers distinguish and ascertain the different Forces, mutual Proportions and Relations, which the Passions bear to each other and to the whole . . . and are capable of directing or restraining the blind Impulses of Passion in a due Consistency one with the other, and a regular Subordination to the whole System.

Fortunately, "Nature has . . . endued us with a MIDDLE FACULTY, wonderfully adapted to our MIXED State, which holds partly of *Sense* and partly of *Reason*," and serves as a kind of storehouse, where the esthetic or ethical sensibility is "refined from its Dross" by mixing with the moral or intellectual. The exercise of this Middle Faculty is not to be expected during our first period of life, when we acquire a sensible or natural taste toward objects which we generally call *good* or *pleasant*, Fordyce cautions. But as the mind develops, receiving a more complex set of ideas, these perceptions are referred to the Middle Faculty to form a higher taste than the sensible and to influence our finer passions toward the harmonious, the great, and the beautiful. In a third stage of development the mind ascends to yet a more complex set of ideas—"the Order, and Mutual Relations of Minds to each other, their reciprocal Affections, Characters, Actions." We call this a Moral Sense, as distinguished from the earlier or Natural Sense.

Though the mind develops, and with it reason or intellect, it never completely transcends the function of the senses. "We perceive the Natures of Things by different Organs or Sences," and as with the maturer Roderick, "our Reason acts upon them when so perceived, and investigates those Relations which subsist between them, or traces what is true, what is false, what may be affirmed, and what denied concerning them. . . ."[16]

REFERENCES

1. One notable exception is Eugene Joliat's *Smollett et la France* (Paris, 1935), a study which has generally been ignored. Joliat develops at length three basic ways in which Smollett's perspective differs from that of Le Sage: "En opposition à un Gil Blas souriant il tâchera de créer un Roderick sérieux. Aux aventures nombreuses du héros de Lesage, aux coups de fortune brusques et peu naturels qui changent en quelques secondes la vie de celui-ci, il opposera une suite d'aventures moins hachées, mieux enchaînées, qui ne sentiront en aucune façon un procédé d'auteur, mais qui auront l'air d'avoir été vécues. Enfin, au lieu de rendre son roman moral en faisant constater, comme Lesage, combien le vice est inutile et ridicule, Smollett s'érigera en moraliste militant et montrera le visage hideux du mal, pour le faire haïr" (p. 35).

2. Hoxie N. Fairchild, *Religious Trends in English Poetry* (New York, 1942), II, 9, 366.

3. Basil Willey, *The Eighteenth-Century Background* (London, 1950), pp. 108-09, 207-08.

4. Lois Whitney, *Primitivism and the Idea of Progress* (Baltimore, 1934), p. 69.

5. David Daiches Raphael, *The Moral Sense* (Oxford, 1947), pp. 1-2.

6. Adam Ferguson, *An Essay on the History of Civil Society* (London, 1773), pp. 47-48.

7. George Turnbull, *Observations upon Liberal Education* (London, 1742), pp. 423-24.

8. Hugh Blair, *Lectures on Rhetoric* (Philadelphia, 1846), pp. 16-25.

9. Adam Smith, *The Theory of Moral Sentiments* (London, 1861), pp. 469-71.

10. Thomas Reid, *Works*, ed. Sir William Hamilton (Edinburgh, 1863), I, 421-25.

11. Many of the contradictions which Whitney, pp. 238-76, seemingly discerns in minor novelists of the period—Robert Bage, Charlotte Smith, Thomas Holcroft, Mary Hays—are clearly the result of *a priori* assumptions about antitheses which have been superimposed upon the works. If these writers are granted their own assumptions, those developed within the matrix of the novels, there is no question about their appearing less contradictory than Whitney's study finds them.

12. Walter Scott, *Lives of Eminent Novelists and Dramatists* (London, n.d.), p. 463.

13. This is confirmed by multiple references throughout. See especially I, 129, where Strap draws a lengthy distinction between Random, who is "born a gentleman," and himself, the "poor but honest cobbler's son." Later (III, 1), invited to dine with Random and his father, Strap properly insists on his place as a social inferior and declines the honor. Smollett's preface emphasizes the reasons for bestowing upon Roderick an education suitable to "the dignity of his birth and character." His grandfather is "a gentleman of considerable fortune and influence" (I, 1); his father speaks of "the dignity and circumstances of his family" (I, 3); Thomson considers his "birth and talents" (II, 42); and Morgan is drawn to him because he is "descended of a good family" (II, 43). As officer aboard the *Thunder*, Roderick is "resolved to maintain the dignity of my station" (II, 52); and when he first meets Narcissa, he admittedly tries to "revolve a hundred schemes for assuming the character of a gentleman, to which I thought myself entitled by birth and education" (II, 151). Social hierarchy is beyond question a major assumption behind *Roderick Random*, a provocative force behind the hero's righteous indignation.

14. Analogous to Smollett's division of the passions into two disparate branches related to ethical values is Lord Kames' observation in *Elements of Criticism* (New York, 1838) that "the production of emotion or passion, resolves itself into a very simple proposition—that we love what is agreeable, and hate what is disagreeable." Kames assumes as self-evident that "a thing must be agreeable or disagreeable, before it can be the object either or love or of hatred." Thus, "if I love a person, it is for good qualities or good offices: if I have resentment against a man, it must be for some injury he has

done me" (pp. 27-28). Dividing the passions in much the same way, James Beattie insists in *Elements of Moral Science* (Philadelphia, 1809) that "desires and aversions are two copious classes of passions; and assume different forms, and are called by different names, according to the nature of good or evil that draws them forth, and its situation with respect to us" (I, 192 ff.).

15. Scott, p. 441. Obviously a paraphrase of Scott is Ernest Baker's contention in *The History of the English Novel* (London, 1930), IV, 202-03, that structure consists of "a string of episodes, with no connection except that they happen to one personage." Lewis M. Knapp also insists in *Tobias Smollett* (Princeton, 1949) that the reader will never "experience a dramatic ordering" of events in *Roderick Random*. "Instead, he will be led through a chain-like linkage of relatively short episodes" (p. 317). Even Rufus Putney, who has offered a most intensive analysis of Smollett's second novel in "The Plan of *Peregrine Pickle*," *PMLA*, LX (1945), 1051-65, differentiates between *Roderick Random* and *Peregrine Pickle*, explaining that the former is only a series of episodes, the history of Roderick's early life, whereas the latter is planned satire.

16. David Fordyce, *Elements of Moral Philosophy*, in Robert Dodsley's *The Preceptor* (London, 1748), II, 248-49, 267-68, 343-47.

CHAPTER THREE. *PEREGRINE PICKLE:*

A Study in Imagination and Judgment

1. IN TURNING to Smollett's second novel, critics have been almost unanimous in discerning, and also condemning, what appears on the surface as pure and unmitigated farce.[1] *The Adventures of Peregrine Pickle,* however, partakes more of wit than farce, and less of the ludicrous than the satiric. The adventures may appear farcical, but only when particular events within the novel are removed from their own context and reflected against a nineteenth-century metaphysics from which we are yet emerging. This is a metaphysics inherently antithetical to eighteenth-century wit and its function relative to the imagination.

Between Addison's approval of wit as a "Resemblance and Congruity of Ideas" and Hazlitt's derision of this fanciful device which simply "adds littleness to littleness" lies an etymological record of the pejorative. More significant, however, close examination of *Spectator Papers No. 58-63* and *Lectures on the Comic Writers* reveals an ideational shift basic to eighteenth- and early nineteenth-century thought. For Addison, wit is closely related to imagination and therefore antithetical to judgment, the vehicle of truth. For Hazlitt and the Romantics in general, however, wit is related to judgment and therefore opposed to imagination, which has become the organ of truth and understanding. This shift is not too remote from the development of the term *nature,* identified with geometric reason during the early part of the century, but assuming connotations of reason's antithesis, the inner feeling, by the later decades. This distinction clearly involves opposing theories of language and laughter in the light of which Smollett's *Peregrine Pickle* is as far removed from the cleverness of Pope's mythic analogues in "The Rape of the Lock" as it is from Lamb's quaint and fanciful reminiscences in "The Praise of Chimney-Sweepers." Correspondingly, this suggests contradictory theories of reality and knowledge, art and values.[2]

In *Spectator No. 58* Addison differentiates between true and false wit—the latter, a result of "great Industry"; the former, of "beautiful Genius." The distinction is of course borrowed from Locke, as Addison concedes in *No. 62:*

> . . . Men who have a great deal of Wit and prompt Memories, have not always the clearest Judgment, or deepest Reason. For Wit lying most in the Assemblage of Ideas, and putting those together with Quickness and Variety, wherein can be found any Resemblance or Congruity, thereby to make up pleasant Pictures and agreeable Visions in the Fancy; Judgment, on the contrary, lies quite on the other Side, In separating carefully one from another, Ideas wherein can be found the least Difference, thereby to avoid being misled by Similitude, and by Affinity to take one thing for another. This is a way of proceeding quite contrary to Metaphor and Allusion; wherein, for the most part, lies that Entertainment and Pleasantry of Wit which strikes so lively on the Fancy, and is therefore so acceptable to all People.

For Addison, as for Locke, true wit is a vehicle of the fancy, ornamental in manner (using "Metaphor and Allusion"); associational in means (through "Assemblage of Ideas"); and emotionally pleasurable in end (resulting in "pleasant Pictures and agreeable Visions"). As a vehicle of the fancy, wit is also to be identified with Addison's secondary pleasures of the imagination (the two terms, *fancy* and *imagination*, are synonymous and interchangeable in Addison)—those pleasures flowing from "Ideas of visible Objects, when the Objects are not actually before the Eye, but are called up into our Memories, or formed into agreeable Visions of Things that are either Absent or Fictitious" (*No. 411*). Like wit, then, which assembles ideas with "Resemblance and Congruity," the secondary pleasures embrace "Resemblance, or at least some remote Analogy. . . . Since it is in the Power of the Imagination, when it is once Stocked with particular Ideas, to enlarge, compound, and vary them at her own Pleasure" (No. 416). Though pleasures of the understanding may be "more preferable, because they are founded on some new Knowledge or Improvement in the Mind of Man; yet it must be confest, that those of the Imagination are as great and as transporting as the other" (No. 411).

Like Bacon and Hobbes before him, who saw the imagination as a "decaying sense" which can give rise only to the fictitious, the falsifying shadow of essences, Addison did not claim for the fancy any means of achieving truths or insights into reality. He insisted merely on her ornamental, associational, and pleasurable powers. Avoiding problems of knowledge and reality, and concentrating instead upon theories of pleasure and sublimity—a change which Hume and Burke were later to reinforce—Addison effectively paved the way for the early Romantics, who were to insist on the validity of the imagination's findings and the truth of its creations.[3] "Imagination, the real & eternal World of which this Vegetable Universe is but a faint shadow," Blake was to write in Jerusalem. Later, Keats was to insist that "what the imagination seizes as Beauty must be truth." And in his essay "On Reason and Imagination" Hazlitt contended that "passion . . . is the essence, the chief ingredient in moral truth; and the warmth of passion is sure to kindle the light of imagination on the objects around it."

Accordingly, when Hazlitt curtly dismisses Peregrine Pickle as a novel which "is no great favourite of mine," he undoubtedly uses evaluative criteria not too remote from those he employs with Pope's or Cowley's lines. Like Cowley, Pope is castigated for developing his lines "with wit and fancy," neither being for Hazlitt qualities of the poetical or the imaginative. Pope's insights, like Cowley's, are "mere dry observation on human life, without elevation or enthusiasm . . . of that quaint and familiar kind that is merely curious and fanciful." Because the function of poetry or imagination is to elevate, to transport, to find truth and beauty in their only realm, the sublime, Hazlitt sees that "wit . . . is the imagination or fancy inverted, and so applied to given objects, as to make the little look less, the mean more light and worthless; or to divert our admiration or wean our affections from that which is lofty and impressive, instead of producing a more intense admiration and exalted passion. . . ." Wit, then, is for Hazlitt antithetical to the imagination, the latter being an elevating and truth-finding faculty, whereas wit hovers about the edges of the light and trivial. Wit for him is only a vehicle for the ludicrous or laughable, whose "essence . . . is the incongruous, the disconnecting one idea from another, or the jostling of one feeling against another." Thus, Addison's and Locke's contention (borrowed from Hobbes), that "wit or ludicrous invention produces its effect oftenest by comparison," is rejected as a half-truth:

> In a word, the shrewd separation or disentangling of ideas that seem the same, or where the secret contradiction is not sufficiently suspected, and is of a ludicrous and whimsical nature, is wit just as much as the bringing together those that appear at first sight totally different. There is then no sufficient ground for admitting Mr. Locke's celebrated definition of wit, which he makes to consist in the finding out striking and unexpected resemblances in things so as to make pleasant pictures in the fancy, while judgment and reason, according to him, lie the clean contrary way, in separating and nicely distinguishing those wherein the smallest difference is to be found.

Because it assumes the function of both comparison and contrast, wit is assigned by Hazlitt the role Addison and Locke had reserved for judgment—though it is made to differ from judgment in the unexpectedness of its connections and in the ensuing laughter. Consequently, wit can be viewed by Hazlitt as an agent of geometric reasoning and false judging powers—forces hostile to the imaginative faculties, which alone are conducive to those sublime truths achieved through art and poetry.

Not until the turn of the century does the imagination, whose role in English neo-classical poetics had been originally inhibited by Bacon and Hobbes, finally come into its own. Although this shift in roles has been attributed to Adam Smith, whose theory of the sympathetic imagination is developed in Hazlitt and echoed by Keats, the influence of the Scottish Common-Sense School, whose views were shared by Smith, must be considered in perceiving the forces at work.[4] By increasingly demanding for the imagination a moral and esthetic role previously sacred to the understanding or judgment, the Scottish writers reveal a major propensity to reconcile the claims of both the imagination and the judgment and to offer a mediating position in the midst of what, for the eighteenth century, was a clashing opposition.

The imagination is obviously an agent of sympathy in Smith's *The Theory of Moral Sentiments:*

> Though our brother is upon the rack, as long as we ourselves are at our ease, our senses will never inform us of what he suffers. They never did, and never can, carry us beyond our own person, and it is by the imagination only that we can form any conception of what are his sensations. . . . It is the impressions of our senses only, not those of his, which our imaginations copy. By the imagination we place ourselves in his situation. . . .

Seemingly, the imagination has appropriated in Smith some of the powers which the empiricists had previously relegated to the senses. But the imagination has also appropriated some of the powers of the understanding, for it is simultaneously a source of judgment. Ideas of justice and propriety stem from "perfect concord with the sympathetic emotions of the spectator," while concepts of injustice and impropriety arise when there is no coincidence between what one feels and the causes which excite the feeling. "To approve of the passions of another, therefore, as suitable to their objects, is the same thing as to observe that we do entirely sympathize with them," Smith writes; "and not to approve of them as such, is the same thing as to observe that we do not entirely sympathize with them."[5]

Similarly, John Ogilvie offers a cogent argument for the unification of imagination and judgment in "An Essay on the Lyric Poetry of the Ancients." True genius, Ogilvie points out, is the offspring of both judgment and imagination, unified, cooperating, and properly moderated. Though a separate province is assigned each faculty, it is most difficult to prevent one from encroaching upon the other and leading to dangerous extremes. The one is uniform, regular, invariable, and permanent; the other is abrupt, spontaneous, and irregular. While the former alone may result in intrinsic excellence, yet it "can never be productive of general improvement, as attention can only be fixed by entertainment, and entertainment is incompatible with unvaried uniformity." On the other hand, "when Imagination is permitted to bestow the graces of ornament indiscriminately, we either find in the general that senti- ments are superficial, and thinly scattered through a work, or we are obliged to search for them beneath a load of superfluous colouring." Such, Ogilvie contends, "is the appearance of the superior Faculties of the mind when they are disunited from each other, or when either of them seems to be remarkably predominant."[6]

Alexander Gerard, too, is insistent upon "the most improved use" of man's faculties in the development of taste, which is depend- ent upon a proper compound of imagination and judgment. "Taste consists chiefly in the improvement of those principles which are commonly called *the powers of imagination,* and are considered by modern philosophers as *internal* or *reflex senses,* supplying us with finer and more delicate perceptions, than any which can be properly referred to our external organs," Gerard contends at the opening of *An Essay on Taste.* The first part of his work is devoted to an analy- sis of these senses—novelty, sublimity, beauty, imitation, harmony, ridicule, virtue—while the remainder of the *Essay* concerns itself with the problem of how these senses cooperate in forming taste, and how judgment must be combined with their exertions to ren- der improvement, for "*goodness* of taste . . . consists in certain *excellences* of our original powers of judgment and imagination combined."[7]

With an acknowledged debt to Gerard's writings, James Beattie observes that "by Imagination, we *invent;* that is, produce arrangements of ideas and objects that were never so arranged be- fore." Imagination is not only capable of invention, however, for "by Imagination, also, in certain cases, we are enabled to *judge*, because qualified to form distinct ideas of those things in nature, art, and science, which exercise our reason, or call forth our affections." Thus, during the course of a dream-state, or during a diseased condition, "imagination often operates with astonishing vivacity: but that is not Genius, because it is not regulated by knowledge or judgment, and tends to no useful purpose." Beattie's remarks in *Dissertations Moral and Critical* are deliberately aimed "with a view to combat an opinion . . . that Genius, especially poetical genius, is nothing more than a certain warmth of fancy, or enthusiasm of mind, which is all-sufficient in itself, and stands in no need of judgment, or good sense, to give it direction and regularity." In a similar fashion Beattie observes that a person of taste—for sublimity or for ridicule, for beauty or for virtue—must possess the following requisites:

> first, a lively and correct imagination; secondly, the power of distinct apprehension; thirdly, the capacity of being easily, strongly, and agreeably affected, with sublimity, beauty, harmony, exact imitation, etc.; fourthly, Sympathy, or Sensibility of heart; and, fifthly, Judgment, or Good Sense, which is the principal thing, and may not very improperly be said to comprehend all the rest.

The function of the individual is not only to apprehend, but to judge; not only to employ the language of enthusiasm and express those passions agitating the soul, but to adjust and correct. "The greatest liveliness of imagination will . . . avail but little, if it is not *corrected* and regulated by the knowledge of nature, both external or material, and internal or moral. Without this, there cannot be Taste; because one cannot discern whether the productions of art . . . be good or bad."[8]

Much of the basis for James Beattie's contentions—like those of Gerard, Ogilvie, Smith, Lord Kames, Hugh Blair, Archibald Alison, Lord Monboddo, and others who formed the nucleus of the Scottish School—can be found in the writings of Francis Hutcheson, frequently viewed as the originator of the Common-Sense philosophy. Though Clarence DeWitt Thorpe has cogently argued that Hutcheson's divergences from Shaftesbury tend to align him more with Locke and Addison, despite the purported aim of *An Inquiry into the Original of our Ideas of Beauty and Virtue* to explain and defend Shaftesbury's principles, Thorpe tends to obscure Hutcheson's position.[9] By stressing Hutcheson's similarity to Locke and Addison and ignoring differences, Thorpe overlooks the possibility for a mediating position of the Scottish School relative to the rationalism of the neo-Platonists and the increasing mechanism of the Lockean empiricists.

Actually, Hutcheson's distinction between the external and the internal senses—the former, the mere sensation of seeing and hearing; the latter, a power of perceiving Beauty, Harmony, Virtue, etc.—bears within it an inherent relationship between the esthetic and the moral, a relationship which the followers of Hutcheson were to develop in strength. Superficially, this distinction seems analogous to Addison's division in *Spectator No. 411* of the Pleasures of the Imagination:

> those Primary Pleasures of the Imagination, which entirely proceed from such Objects as are [before our] Eye[s]; and . . . those Secondary Pleasures of the Imagination which flow from the Ideas of visible Objects, when the Objects are not actually before the Eye, but are called up into our Memories, or formed into agreeable Visions of Things that are either Absent or Fictitious.

But the end of Addison's esthetic is in the pleasurable emotions which result from the experience, the agreeableness of the vision which can transport the observer into the realm of sublimity. Hutcheson, however, recognizes that "the violent Pursuit of the Pleasures of the *external Senses*, or *Sensuality*, is opposite to the Pleasure of the *Imagination*," and that "the violent Pursuits of either of the former kinds of Pleasure, is often directly inconsistent with public *Affections*, and with our *moral Sense*, and *Sense of Honour*." Thus, in defending Shaftesbury against the attacks of Mandeville, Hutcheson obviously found it essential to differentiate between those esthetic pleasures which we desire for ourselves and those which we desire for others, selfish pleasures and public or benevolent pleasures. Because our desire or aversion for them is coincident with the formation of an idea of objects or events, he writes in *An Essay on the Nature and Conduct of the Passions and Affections,* "Consequently our Affections must very much depend upon the Opinions we form, concerning any thing which occurs to our Mind." These are opinions which can be formed and developed by education and training, by association with "Persons of *corrected Imaginations*" who aim at virtue. "If just *Reflection* comes in, and tho' late, applies the proper Cure, by correcting the *Opinions* and the *Imagination,* every Experience will tend to our Advantage."[10]

It is somewhat moot whether Hutcheson and the Scottish School which inherited his ideas are more closely aligned with the morality of Shaftesbury and the rational esthetics of the seventeenth-century Platonists or with the theories of sublimity emanating out of Locke and Addison. As long as we assume an irreconcilable clash between these two views, then the ideologies of Addison and Hazlitt, like those of the "neo-classicists" and the "romantics" in general, must be interpreted as dichotomous and irrevocably opposed. If, on the other hand, we accept possibilities of a middle ground, then an ideational matrix can be envisioned for the century in which judgment is set in only varying degrees of opposition to wit and the imagination.

Against this ideational matrix, established by Hutcheson and developed by men like Smith, Ogilvie and Gerard, the seemingly "farcical adventures" of *Peregrine Pickle* are seen to their best advantage. Peregrine, whose "disposition broke out into those irregularities and wild sallies of a luxuriant imagination" (I, 151), is revealed early in the novel as a boy who is "almost incessantly laying traps for diversion at his neighbour's expense" (II, 99). The search for "diversion" is frequently expressed in mischievous pranks. But Peregrine also manifests a "satirical disposition [which] was never more gratified than when he had an opportunity of expos-

ing grave characters in ridiculous attitudes" (I, 146). By the close
of the novel, the unrestrained pursuit of pleasures through the
imagination having led the protagonist to personal chaos and social
isolation, he learns to temper the excessive fancy with judgment and
reveals "surprising temperance; everybody was charmed with his
affability and moderation" (IV, 263). Here, *wit* and *imagination*
and their ultimate relationship to *judgment,* adhere neither to Addison's nor Hazlitt's conception. Textual analysis reveals that they oc-
cupy a medial and reconciling position, more closely allied to the
moral and esthetic standards of the Scottish Common-Sense School.

2. LIKE RODERICK RANDOM, Peregrine Pickle is endowed
with strong antithetical passions. He is revealed as "naturally generous" (I, 152), "naturally compassionate" (II, 13), with "a fund
of good-nature" (I, 79), "unlimited generosity" (I, 116), and "natural benevolence" (I, 184). He displays a "generous passion" (I,
118) and "ideas of generosity [that] were extremely refined" (I,
174). "A professed enemy to all oppression" (II, 36), he extends
"his generosity and compassion to the humble and needy" (IV, 3),
revealing "that compassion and complaisance which was natural
to his disposition" (IV, 38), even in the depths of depravity to
which he eventually sinks.

   These social passions are both natural and abundant. But Peregrine is also endowed with unsocial feelings which increase, as the
novel progresses, so that before long he is "torn by conflicting passions; love, shame, and remorse, contended with vanity, ambition,
and revenge." His soul gravitates between the social and the unsocial, "each of these passions equally turbulent and loud in demanding gratification" (III, 42-46). As a child, despite natural
benevolence, he also develops "pride . . . licentious conduct
. . . [and] contracted a large proportion of insolence" (I, 79). At
fourteen, "vanity took the lead of his passions," and though he

follows "the genuine dictates of his heart" in his initial meetings
with Emilia, news of her frugal means "alarmed his pride" and
caused a "struggle between his interest and love." Emilia herself
discerns "in the midst of all his tenderness, a levity of pride" (I, 116-
24); while Gam, his treacherous brother, jealously plots to "muti-
late him in such a manner, that he should have no cause to be vain
of his person for the future" (I, 208). Though generosity and compassion are Peregrine's major virtues, increasingly "vanity and pride
were the ruling foibles of our adventurer" (III, 23).

In *Roderick Random* the antithetical passions were an immediate prelude to action, and therefore the novel teemed with violence,
disorder, and a rapidity of movement. In *Peregrine Pickle* the conflicting passions are first seized by a fertile but irregular imagination, which diverts the passions, with small discrimination, toward
its own ends. Peregrine's passions frequently erupt into "irregularities and wild sallies of a luxuriant imagination" (I, 151), and in no
time he becomes distinguished for his "fertility of fancy" (I, 107).

At times the imagination is socially oriented. Peregrine's initial
affection for Commodore Trunnion, his uncle and godfather, is "if
not produced, at least riveted, by . . . Peregrine's imagination"
(I, 86). After his first meeting with Emilia, he lies awake all night
with plans "his imagination suggested" (I, 120), and before long
he produces stanzas in her praise, for he is totally engrossed by his
amiable mistress, who, whether he slept or waked, was still present
in his imagination" (I, 129). In a later reunion, with "a thousand
fond images recurring to his imagination," he feels his soul dis-
solve into tenderness and love, and confesses "that his imagination
had been haunted by the ideas of Emilia" (IV, 14-19).

More frequently, however, the undisciplined imagination, dictated by pride and vanity, pursues self-interests. Through pride, "his
warm imagination had exaggerated all his own prospects" (I, 122);
therefore, he soon finds Emilia wanting, when he learns she is
without visible dependence. Before long, he entertains "gaudy
schemes of pomp and pleasure, which his luxuriant imagination

had formed" (I, 181). Parting from Emilia, he quickly expels "the melancholy images that took possession of his fancy . . . [and] he called in the flattering ideas of those pleasures he expected to enjoy in France; and, before he had rode ten miles, his imagination was effectually amused" (I, 194). Abroad, he soon forgets Emilia, for "his imagination was engrossed by conquests that more agreeably flattered his ambition" (II, 44).

The imagination is a pleasurable associative power for Peregrine, expressive of these conflicting passions. But it is also a creative and inventive faculty, consistently identified with "genius."[11] Invariably, Perry is alluded to as a master of "invention," possessing "ingenuity" and "talent." Although his imaginative genius is occasionally directed toward creative and socially-oriented goals, for the main part it is destructive and anti-social. It aims at pleasure and diversion, diffusing itself through mischievous pranks and ludicrous jokes, rather than through any esthetic or moral vehicle. He takes "great pleasure" in accidentally treading on his uncle's gout-ridden toe, stealing and burning his tobacco pouches, tweaking his nose, emptying a snuff-box into his favorite beverage. As Smollett himself writes, "it would be an endless, and perhaps no very agreeable task, to enumerate all the unlucky pranks he played upon his uncle and others, before he attained the fourth year of his age" (I, 74). Aided by Hatchway and Pipes, Perry indulges in a "variety of mischievous pranks" (I, 101). The desire for self-amusement rarely leaves him, even as he grows older. Always, he is an "unrelenting wag" (II, 93), a "mischievous youth" (IV, 50), "the mischievous Pickle" (IV, 92) who seeks incessant "diversion at his neighbour's expense" (II, 99). Always he reveals "mischievous intent" (IV, 119), as some "mischievous plan . . . entered our hero's imagination" (IV, 3). Indeed his surname is itself indicative of his *pickled* disposition, with the meaning, now obsolete, which that word assumed, mainly during the eighteenth century, of being mischievous or roguish.[12]

These pranks are a major vehicle of the fancy, diverting and amusing Peregrine, even while discomforting others. But the fertile imagination has at its disposal a second vehicle—what is called alternately "wit" or "satire" or "ridicule." This "strong propensity to contemptuous ridicule" is described in Smollett's *The Present State of All Nations* as "the genuine characteristic of the English people . . . [which is] diffused through the whole nation, from the highest peer to the lowest chimney sweeper."[13] In a sense, certainly, Peregrine Pickle is projected as the typical Englishman, just as the essay prefatory to *Roderick Random* projects its hero as the typical Scot. Smollett notes that "Peregrine's satirical disposition was never more gratified than when he had an opportunity of exposing grave characters in ridiculous attitudes" (I, 146), for "practical satire [is] . . . agreeable and peculiar to his disposition" (III, 228). Even as an infant, he would cry out for his phlegmatic father and malicious mother, and then "lie sprawling and laughing in their faces, as if he ridiculed the impertinence of their concern"; and the commodore, whose "social passions of the soul . . . were strangely warped, disguised, and overborne," is marked out early in the boy's life "as a proper object of ridicule, for almost all his little childish satire was levelled against him" (I, 72-73). At Winchester School he exercises his talents against his pedantic tutor:

> Scarcely a day passed in which he did not find means to render Mr.
> Jolter the object of ridicule; his violent prejudices, ludicrous vanity,
> awkward solemnity, and ignorance of mankind, afforded continual
> food for the raillery, petulance, and satire of his pupil, who never
> neglected an opportunity of laughing, and making others laugh at
> his expense. (I, 107)

At Oxford, Perry attaches himself to a club of political reformers, "because he perceived ample subject for his ridicule, in the characters of these wrong-headed enthusiasts" (I, 145).

While the satire and ridicule rise from a love of moral virtue, they generally aim at the same pleasures and diversions as the mischievous pranks. Subjects for the pranks are indiscriminately chosen, but subjects for the ridicule are carefully selected from the foibles of those who surround him: his malicious parents, the grotesque Trunnion, the pedantic Jolter, the political enthusiasts. In his capacity as narrator, Smollett structures Peregrine's satirical disposition for his own esthetic ends, but these are to be distinguished from Peregrine's. Indeed, the disparity between Smollett's use of satire as a means of learning, and Peregrine's as a means of self-amusement, points to the central failing of the protagonist's wild and irregular imagination—its increasing demand for pleasure, oblivious of social and moral values.

Prompted by pride and ambition, the imagination can hurl the protagonist in pursuit of love, its pleasures and amusements; similarly, vanity can hurl the imagination in pursuit of laughter through wit and satire. Unfortunately, Peregrine's imaginative genius leads him increasingly in pursuit of his own appetites and interests. Love gives way before lust; laughter, before contempt. Peregrine's fertile imagination is wild and undisciplined, and lacks regularity—and "to render genius complete, fertility and regularity of imagination must be united," as the novelist's Scottish contemporary, Alexander Gerard, points out, for "their union forms that boundless penetration which characterizes true genius."[14] Coupled with the conflicting and antithetical passions, and without any directing or judging power, the fertile imagination in Peregrine necessarily runs rampant, since it lacks both decorum and discretion.

3. EFFORTS ARE consistently made to develop Peregrine's potential for a directing and harmonizing judgment, but he alternates throughout the first section of the novel (chs. I-XXXIV) between the possibilities of harmony and the realities of diversity.

One of the major obstacles to the development of any unifying force here is the morally bifurcated universe confronting Peregrine from the outset and contributing to inner conflicting passions. During much of his childhood, young Peregrine alternates between

the household of his malicious parents and that of his benevolent
uncle. "Little subject to refined sensations" and "scarce ever dis-
turbed with violent emotions of any kind," his father is phlegmatic
and sluggish; he is "never known to betray the faintest symptom of
transport" (I, 2-3). On the other hand, his uncle, Hawser Trunnion, is frequently "thrown into perilous passions and quandaries,"
when he storms like a perfect hurricane (I, 6-7). Both men are
dominated by their wives. Whereas Trunnion's subjection is "like
that of a bear, chequered with fits of surliness and rage," Pickle
bears his yoke "like an ox, without repining" (I,140). In the household of his natural parents, Peregrine encounters "unnatural
caprice" and "virulence of . . . hate" (I, 104), "unnatural aversion," "unnatural prejudice," and "unnatural barbarity" (II, 217-
24). The father's apathy and the mother's malice are generally
"frustrated by the love and generosity of Trunnion, who, having
adopted him as his own son" (I, 104), proceeds to lavish upon him
an "affection [which] rose to such a pitch of enthusiasm, that he
verily believed him to be the issue of his own loins." Even Mrs.
Trunnion's affection for Perry increases "in the same proportion
as his own mother's diminished . . . so that Peregrine, as on the
one hand he was abhorred, so on the other was he caressed" (I,
138-39). Peregrine is aware of this confusing world into which he
has been thrust, for as he himself points out, with Trunnion he is
"on the footing of an orphan, who depends entirely upon his
benevolence"; whereas with his parents, who are "obliged to provide for me by the ties of nature, as well as the laws of the land,"
he can depend only upon a large store of enmity and rancour
(I, 179).

Even before Peregrine is removed completely to the garrison
—the commodore's nautical habitation, which Sterne later adapted
for Uncle Toby—his talents are nurtured by Trunnion's companions, Pipes and Hatchway. Delighting "in superintending the first
essays of his genius," they develop the boy's tendency toward
mischief and satire, by both instruction and example.

At the age of four, he is sent to a neighboring day school, but there "he made little progress, except in mischief, which he practised with impunity." Not until he is removed to a boarding school near London, away from the influence of Pipes and Hatchway, and separated from his malicious mother and jejune father, does the boy abandon, even temporarily, his desire for amusement. Within a year, through the aid of his new tutor, Mr. Jennings, he becomes remarkable for his brightness. His "genius and ambition" are kindled, and he loses "all relish for diversion" (I, 73-77). Before long, however, the love for amusement revives and alternates with his newly-formed love for learning. Because the commodore discerns that the pranks are "rather the effect of wantonness than malice" and Peregrine's "genius . . . would be lost for want of cultivation" (I, 102), he hires Mr. Jolter for a tutor and settles his nephew at Winchester School. Here, too, the lad's abilities in learning are developed, for Peregrine proves himself not "deficient in the more solid accomplishments of youth; he had profited in his studies beyond expectation, and besides that sensibility of discernment which is the foundation of taste . . . he had already given several specimens of a very promising poetic talent" (I, 116). Here too, though, especially since Pipes accompanies him as an attendant, and Hatchway is allowed periodic visits, "prank succeeded prank, and outrage followed outrage, with surprising velocity" (I, 110). When his nephew is seventeen, the commodore resolves to "send him to the university, where his education might be completed, and his fancy weaned from all puerile amusements" (I, 135). When this proves insufficient, he determines "to send the young gentleman on his travels, in the course of which he would, in all probability, forget the amusements of his greener years" (I, 180).

The commodore reveals one dominant aim in each attempt at educating young Peregrine: to curb the undisciplined fancy which abandons itself to diversity and pleasures, and to develop the harmonizing and socially-oriented faculty of judgment.

Ironically, Hawser Trunnion is himself guilty of misjudgment in his determination to send Peregrine abroad. True, the Grand

Tour was somewhat a fad during the century, and young gentlemen commonly traveled for improvement, after studying at a university.[15] But greater potentialities for Peregrine's improvement lie in England at this time, and not on the Continent.

Trunnion has misjudged the influence of Emilia. Her meeting with Peregrine occurs when his social passions are most at conflict with the unsocial, and his good humor most contending with unbridled levity for expression, so that "his character thus wavered between the ridicule of some and the regard of others." Fortunately, her meeting with Peregrine while he is at Winchester, "by contracting his view to one object, detached him from those vain pursuits that would in time have plunged him into an abyss of folly and contempt" (I, 117). Undeniably, she exerts a good influence upon young Perry. The Trunnions, who know of Emilia only through the officious Mr. Jolter, regard her as "that girl who has seduced his youth" (I, 174), as one of his many "puerile amusements" (I, 135), as "a painted galley, which will decoy you upon the flats of destruction" (I, 175).

The trip abroad, far from diminishing Peregrine's pursuit of amusements and self-interests, appeals directly to his unsocial passions. His imagination "was perfectly well pleased with the prospect of going abroad, which flattered his vanity and ambition." With little foresight, he does not "believe a short absence would tend to the prejudice of his love, but, on the contrary, enhance the value of his heart"; however, Emilia herself "had discernment enough to foresee, that vanity or interest, co-operating with the levity of youth, might one day deprive her of her lover" (I, 181-84).

In effect, Trunnion's well-meaning but misguided benevolence poses for his nephew a set of false alternatives: either the boy abandon his "painted galley" and go abroad, or he must expect a cessation of the commodore's generosity and assistance. What begins as Hawser Trunnion's misjudgment culminates in vital error and indiscretion on the part of Peregrine himself. Because Perry chooses to retain the commodore's affection, he abandons Emilia and agrees to the Grand Tour. From this point he moves, with increasing rapidity, toward the aggrandizement of self-interest, while pursuing the pleasures of his imagination.

4. THIS FIRST SECTION of the novel reveals the extravagantly imaginative youth, alternating between the malicious Pickles and the benevolent Trunnions, between mischievous pranks and moral learning, between pedantic tutors and the affectionate Emilia. Within the second section (chs. XXXV-C) the excesses of his luxuriant imagination rapidly develop the unsocial passions. Pride and folly surge to their height, as the wild and unrestrained fancy leads him increasingly to artifice and self-amusement, a danger both to himself and society. Through his own defect in judgment, Peregrine manages to remove himself, before the close of this middle section, from all social virtues.

The greatest impediments to narrative flow within this middle section are the two lengthy *historiettes,* "The Memoirs of a Lady of Quality" (ch. LXXXI), and the account of Mr. Mackercher (ch. XCVIII). Together, these account for almost a fourth of the entire novel. Recognized immediately upon publication as the confessions of the notorious Lady Vane, the "Memoirs" assured a rapid and sensational success for the novel, though, as Saintsbury points out in his preface, the two episodic chapters "are probably at least as damaging now as they were once helpful to that popularity." Composition of Lady Vane's narrative is generally ascribed to her, but corrections and revisions in the second and somewhat expurgated edition were provided by Smollett himself.[16] Smollett's hand is visible most perceptibly in the opening paragraphs of the "Memoirs," which establish a link with the central ethical theme: the excessive imagination, which is as crucial to Lady Vane's life as it is to Peregrine's adventures. The "Lady of Quality," like Peregrine Pickle, is much addicted to a "love of pleasure [which] . . . encouraged those ideas of vanity and ambition which spring up so early in the human mind." Like Pickle, she is "lively and good-

natured," and possesses an "imagination apt to run riot" (III, 74).
Precisely the same kind of link is established for the life of Mr.
Mackercher who, like the hero of the novel, is "left an orphan to
the care of an uncle." Mackercher is also carried away by the excesses of his fancy, for "his imagination was so heated by the warlike
achievements he found recorded in the Latin authors . . . that he
was seized with an irresistible thirst of military glory" (IV, 153 ff.).

These two episodic chapters are unrelated to the organic development of the central plot, though opening paragraphs of both
interpolations do provide some link with the running narrative.
Like the tale of Miss Williams in *Roderick Random*, these sections
obviously aim at reinforcing Smollett's moral theme and at providing a cautionary note for the errant protagonist. Although these
interpolations do lend thematic reinforcement, they also weaken
architectonics by detracting from the development of the protagonist, which has been so carefully charted in the opening section of
the novel. If they can be temporarily disregarded in considering the
middle section, then three stages of Peregrine's disintegration
become manifest.

During the Grand Tour, in the first stage of Peregrine's de-
terioration (chs. XXXV-LXV), the fertile imagination seeks only
the pleasures of diversity, as Peregrine concentrates all his talents
upon love and wit. "His vanity suggested, that now the time was
come when he should profit by his talents among the fair sex, on
whom he resolved to employ his utmost art and address." Therefore
he assiduously cultivates a nobleman friend and "for some time,
shared in all his amusements" (II, 32). The influence of Emilia is
forgotten before long, for "his imagination was engrossed by conquests that more agreeably flattered his ambition." He becomes
preoccupied with Mrs. Hornbeck, with the fair Fleming from
Brussels, and with a multiplicity of lesser amours:

> His vanity had, by this time, disapproved of the engagement he had
> contracted in the rawness and inexperience of youth, suggesting that
> he was born to make such an important figure in life as ought to
> raise his ideas above the consideration of any such middling con-

nexions, and fix his attention upon objects of the most sublime attraction. These dictates of ridiculous pride had almost effaced the remembrance of his amiable mistress—or, at least, so far warped his morals and integrity, that he actually began to conceive hopes of her altogether unworthy of his own character, and her deserts. (II, 44)

When his imagination is not anticipating the pleasures of artful conquests in love, it amuses itself in conquering the ridiculous foibles of those who surround him. Primarily, the ridicule is focused upon Mr. Jolter, his governor and companion throughout the Tour; and upon a physician and a painter, whose acquaintance he cultivates because he sees in them "an infinite fund of diversion." He knows he can "amuse himself at their expense in his journey through Flanders" (II, 56). All three are fitting subjects for his satirical disposition, and more than half the journey is given over to an accumulation of static incidents, as Perry successfully pits one against the other in his search for amusement. Of Jolter, the Tory pedant, and the physician, a Whig enthusiast, it is observed:

> These gentlemen, with an equal share of pride, pedantry, and saturnine disposition, were, by the accidents of education and company, diametrically opposite in political maxims; the one . . . being a bigoted high churchman, and the other a rank republican. It was an article of the governor's creed, that the people could not be happy, nor the earth yield its fruits in abundance, under a restricted clergy and limited government; whereas, in the doctor's opinion, it was an eternal truth, that no constitution was so perfect as the democracy, and that no country could flourish, but under the administration of the mob. (II, 61)

The disparity between Smollett's structural intent (to provide Pickle with increasing amusement through his imagination) and his satirical intent (to provoke the reader with learning through moral satire) brings action almost to a halt, as Perry provokes his companions into open conflict in the fields of art, poetry, politics, morals, drama, and antiquarian learning. Although the analysis by Rufus Putney overlooks the antithesis between imagination and judgment which directs the satire toward a larger goal within its eighteenth-century framework, his conclusions about the novel are pertinent:

> It is clear that Smollett's moral obliquity and the structural inadequacies of *Peregrine Pickle* have been exaggerated. . . . Besides entertaining his contemporaries with a series of amusing though undramatic and asymmetrical novels, he showed them their foibles, follies, and vices with a clarity and completeness surpassed only by Hogarth.[17]

Before the Grand Tour, the luxuriant imagination alternated between ideas of mischief and social virtues, amusement and learning. In France, wit and fancy are employed more than either heart or head in pursuit of the pleasures of diversity. Upon Peregrine's return to England, however, pride leads the imagination into open warfare against society. Defying laws of order and gradation, Peregrine's excess becomes now a social sin as well as a personal failing, a crime against *lex continui*—a vice which the eighteenth century consistently deplored.

This second stage (chs. LXVI-LXXXVI), with Peregrine again on English soil after an absence of a year and a half, finds him "dilated with the proud recollection of his own improvement." This improvement, however, is more imaginary than real, for what the fancy sees as progress is in reality degeneration. Lacking in judgment, it cannot perceive a "degeneracy in the sentiments of our imperious youth, who was now in the heyday of his blood, flushed with the consciousness of his own qualifications, vain of his fortune, and elated on the wings of imaginary expectation" (II, 216-17).

With Emilia he now suffers "no emotion but that of vanity and pride, favoured with an opportunity of self-gratification." What before had given rise to tenderness and affection, now provokes his insatiable appetite; "instead of awful veneration, which her presence used to inspire, that chastity of sentiment, and delicacy of expression, he now gazed upon her with the eyes of a libertine, he glowed with the impatience of desire, talked in a strain that barely kept within the bounds of decency" (II, 228-29). His genius is diverted to wile and craftiness. With a political cunning that closely parallels Fathom's Hobbesian *bellum omnium contra omnes*, he commences a "siege" against Emilia with "hypocrisy" and "flattering arts." Cautious that "he might not overshoot himself," he hopes to entangle her heart "within his snares." Setting "his genius at work to invent some scheme" for satisfying his passions, this "insidious lover" attempts to "storm the fort by vigorous assault" (III, 28 ff.). When Peregrine is defeated in his nefarious schemes, he is reduced first to madness and then to physical insensibility, "so much was his imagination engrossed by the prospect of having Emilia in his power" (III, 49).

The unbridled imagination causes him to lose his wits in satire, as well as love. Before, he had sought only gentle amusement; now, he seeks his pleasures in castigation. He forges an entry in Mr. Jolter's pretentious journal; an act that previously might have been intended for his own amusement is now done "by way of punishing the author" (II, 219). With Emilia's brother, Godfrey, he projects "a plan for punishing those villanous pests of society, who prey upon their fellow-creatures" (II, 236), the gamblers and sharpers at Bath. He increasingly identifies himself with the misanthropic Cadwallader Crabtree, who admittedly appears "in the world, not as a member of any community, or what is called a social creature, but merely as a spectator, who entertains himself" with the ridiculous foibles of others: "the crazed Tory, the bigot Whig, the sour, supercilious pedant, the petulant critic, the blustering coward, the fawning tool, the pert imp, sly sharper, and every other species of knaves and fools." Crabtree detects in Peregrine's disposition "a rooted contempt for the world, [which has] made some successful efforts in exposing one part of it to the ridicule of the other," and he suggests an alliance "in prosecuting other schemes of the same nature" (III, 8-15). Since Peregrine, following the failure of his insidious intrigue with Emilia, is anxious "to plunge himself headlong into some intrigue, that might engage his passions and amuse

his imagination" (III, 60), he enters into an alliance with the
man-hating and splenetic Crabtree.

At this crucial point, as Peregrine allies himself with the
misanthrope, "The Memoirs of a Lady of Quality" is inserted into
the narrative. Despite the cautionary note provided by this interlude, the imagination proceeds unimpeded, and Peregrine joins
with Crabtree in concerting "measures for inflicting some dis-
graceful punishment on the shameless and insatiate" (III, 235).
The confederates join wits. Together, "by divers ingenious con-
trivances," they punish "the most flagrant offenders with as much
severity as the nature of their plan would allow" (III, 252). Smollett notes of Peregrine that "had the executive power of the legisla-
ture been vested in him, he would have doubtless devised strange
species of punishment for all offenders against humanity and decorum." Now, however, he "never let slip one opportunity of
mortifying villany and arrogance" and "not only acted the reformer,
or rather the castigator, in the fashionable world, but also exercised
his talents among the inferior class of people, who chanced to incur
his displeasure" (IV, 3).

In the third stage of Peregrine's moral disintegration (chs.
LXXXVII-C) the excesses of an unrestrained imagination, which
previously had led him from amused diversion to contemptuous
laughter, now carry him to the height of his folly—isolated from
society, and seeking within his own fancy the pleasures he cannot
pursue outside of self. This time, however, the degeneration is attended by a reversal in situation that accelerates the moral decline.
His fortune is dissipated; his gaiety diminishes; he is satiated with
pleasures; he moves toward isolation and solitude, ignored by his
friends, outwitted by his enemies.

An unfortunate episode with the "Nymph of the Road"—an
adventure anticipating Shaw's *Pygmalion*—leaves the protagonist
"disgraced among the modest part of his female acquaintance."
Now "free of all female connexions," deprived of the Trunnions
by their deaths, removed from Emilia through his own indiscre-
tions, estranged from his friend Godfrey, Peregrine commences a

"course of fast living among the bucks of the town, and performed innumerable exploits among whores, bullies, rooks, constables, and justices of the peace" (IV, 34-37). Soon, the fortune he has inherited from the commodore is lost: by investments in horse-racing, by extravagant parties, through mortgaging a nobleman's lands, by an abortive effort at entering politics, by standing security to strangers. He is egregiously outwitted in every case. Before long, reduced to writing translations and satirical pieces, he is "determined to profit, in some shape or other, by those talents which he owed to nature and education" (IV, 85). Even his friendship with Crabtree disintegrates, for their intimacy "was now chequered with many occasional tifts, owing to the sarcastic remonstrances of the misanthrope, who disapproved of those schemes which miscarried with Peregrine." He curses "his own folly and extravagance, by which he was reduced to such an uncomfortable situation. . . . He was abandoned by his gaiety and good-humour, his countenance gradually contracted itself into a representation of severity and care, he dropped all his amusements and the companions of his pleasure . . ." (IV, 60-65). Even the last remnants of his generosity and wit are now strangely distorted. "He seemed to confound the ideas of virtue and vice; for he did good, as other people do evil, by stealth; and was so capricious in point of behaviour, that frequently, in public, he wagged his tongue in satirical animadversions upon that poverty which his hand had in private relieved" (IV, 48). In the attempt to retrieve some of his money from Sir Steady Steerwell, he deviates so far from discretion that he is charged with madness. Observers find that "his imagination teems with some extravagant reverie" (IV, 123). Finally, a satirical essay, written in the heat of revenge, arouses the ire of Sir Steady and causes his arrest for outstanding debts.

Bitterly, he rejoices in the knowledge that "a jail is the best tub to which a cynic philosopher can retire," for "in being detached from the world, I shall be delivered from folly and ingratitude." At first, he intends searching "in my own breast for that peace and contentment, which I have not been able to find in all the scenes of my success" (IV, 133). But, "compelled to seek for satisfaction within himself," he refuses the friendly aid of Hatchway and Pipes, becomes alienated from Crabtree, and removes himself from the rest of the prisoners "with an equal abhorrence of the world and himself":

> the more his misery increased, the more haughty and inflexible he became. . . . He was gradually irritated by his misfortunes into a rancorous resentment against mankind in general, and his heart so alienated from the enjoyments of life, that he did not care how soon he quitted his miserable existence. . . . He was even more cautious than ever of incurring obligations; he now shunned his former messmates, in order to avoid disagreeable tenders of friendship . . . and at length secluded himself from all society. (IV, 230-32)

5. ALIENATION from worldly enjoyments is an understandable consequence of Peregrine's excessive imagination. Having indulged itself increasingly in its own pleasures, the imagination has moved him farther and farther away from social virtues. This is a satiety engendered by his own lack of judgment, nurtured by his fertile fancy, encouraged by Trunnion's misjudgment, abetted by Cadwallader's misanthropy, prompted by misfortune, and necessitated by his final imprisonment.

It has been argued, and rightly, that even amid his excesses, Perry manages to maintain the reader's goodwill. If we still display active sympathy for the protagonist, despite his excesses, it is only because we know that he still retains a fund of generosity and benevolence. We know that his excess stems not from any selfish principle within his own constitution—as with Count Fathom, who early adopts a Hobbesian code—but rather from his misdirected choice in seeking his happiness.

Peregrine reveals an abundance of the social passions from the opening section of the novel. His education, thoughtfully provided by the commodore, develops a potential for moral judgment—though immaturity and inexperience preclude any immediate control of the irregular fancy. Without the unifying and harmonizing force which only the fully developed judgment can provide, Peregrine is led increasingly toward diversity and variety. Invention is perverted; genius becomes destructive.

This potentiality for moral judgment is not neglected in the middle section of the novel. Though a more skillful writer might have plotted its decline with a ratio inverse to the ascent of folly, Smollett—with small discrimination, and with little regard for the progress of the imagination—clumsily inserts consistent reminders of his hero's moral potential. As early as his arrival in France, when the "imagination was engrossed" in the conquest of Mrs. Hornbeck, we are reminded that "no man was more capable of moralising upon Peregrine's misconduct than himself; his reflections were extremely just and sagacious, and attended with no other disadvantage but that of occurring too late" (II, 44). When the British ambassador extricates him from a series of catastrophes into which his wit and passion have thrust him, Peregrine is sage enough in "acknowledging the indiscretion of his own conduct" (II, 98). In his affair with the capuchin's companion en route to Brussels, he is reduced almost to delirium by his passion, and must of necessity visit the sights of the city "in order to divert his imagination"—though a renunciatory note soon "banished all remains of discretion from the mind of our hero" (II, 166). After Emilia succeeds in avoiding "the fertility of his invention" (III, 43), and the wild frenzy of his passion has been tamed by illness, he is brought "to a serious consideration of his conduct":

> In this humiliation of his spirits, he reflected with shame and remorse upon his treachery to the fair, the innocent Emilia; he remembered his former sentiments in her favour, as well as the injunctions of his dying uncle; he recollected his intimacy with her brother, against which he had so basely sinned; and, revolving all the circumstances of her conduct, found it so commendable, spirited, and noble, that he deemed her an object of sufficient dignity to merit his honourable addresses, even though his duty had not been concerned in the decision. (III, 55)

Although Emilia's pride precludes any kind of reconciliation, he undergoes a temporary reformation: he "moralised like an apostle, and projected several prudential schemes for his future conduct" (III, 58). Nevertheless, he is soon engrossed in new "amusements . . . among a set of young noblemen, who had denounced war against temperance, economy, and common-sense," and who meet at a tavern "which might be properly styled the Temple of Excess." Even as he resigns himself to these excesses, we are reminded that "Peregrine, in his heart, detested those abandoned courses":

> heated with wine, misled by example, invited on one hand, and defied on the other, [he] forgot all his maxims of caution and sobriety, and, plunging into the reigning folly of the place, had frequent occasions to moralise in the morning upon the loss of the preceding night.
>
> These penitential reflections were attended with many laudable resolutions of profiting by the experience which he had so dearly purchased; but he was one of those philosophers who always put off, till another day, the commencement of their reformation.   (IV, 6-8)

Throughout the middle section of the novel, Smollett plants constant reminders of Peregrine's "intervening checks of Reason." Unfortunately, Perry's remonstrances only allow him to enjoy life more readily, for they "whet his appetite for a repetition of the pleasures . . . so prudently condemned" (IV, 9). Even while hurling him to the height of folly, these moral reflections reinforce our own faith in the protagonist's virtues. As a result, when he eventually faces a recognition of his own excesses during the final movement of the novel (chs. CI-CV), the change is neither unanticipated nor improbable.

Secluded from society, misanthropic, alienated from life's enjoyments, Peregrine suddenly encounters two events in quick succession which provide renewed faith in social bonds. The first is the unexpected appearance of Godfrey Gauntlet, who reveals "the genuine effect of eager gratitude and disinterested love." Godfrey pleads for a reconciliation, expresses gratitude for the benevolence bestowed secretly upon him, and wants to rescue Pickle from his melancholy situation "in spite of yourself." And Peregrine's "heart began to relent accordingly" (IV, 237).

Even while Godfrey is persuading his friend to accept his aid and re-enter society, a grateful letter arrives from Benjamin Chintz, who proposes to repay a seven-hundred-pound debt, for which Perry has already abandoned all hope. This display of integrity and gratitude provides, as Peregrine himself explains, "a more convincing argument . . . than all the casuists in the universe can advance." Once more he becomes "reconciled . . . to life, and disposed . . . to enjoying the comforts of society." Peregrine "renews his Connexion with Society" almost immediately. He reconciles himself with Pipes and Hatchway, and considers plans to alter his behavior (IV, 239-41).

The misanthropic Crabtree offers one kind of plan, that Perry "retire with him to the country, where he might live absolutely independent, and entertain himself, as usual, with the ridiculous characters of mankind." Since Crabtree proposes only a continuation of prior follies, he is stringently opposed by Godfrey, who "objected to this retirement, as a scheme that would blast the fairest promises of fame and fortune, and bury his youth and talents in solitude and obscurity." As for Peregrine himself, "his imagination involuntarily teemed with more agreeable ideas . . . and he could not help forming plans of pastoral felicity in the arms of the lovely Emilia, remote from those pompous scenes which he now detested and despised."

> He amused his fancy with the prospect of being able to support her in a state of independency. . . . He even parcelled out his hours among the necessary cares of the world, the pleasures of domestic bliss, and the enjoyments of a country life; and spent the night in ideal parties with his charming bride, sometimes walking by the sedgy bank of some transparent stream, sometimes pruning the luxuriant vine, and sometimes sitting in social converse with her in a shady grove of his own planting.

These new plans are to substitute the "pleasures of domestic bliss" for the amusements of gallantry and ridicule, and to seek "the enjoyments of a country life" in preference to the entertainments of a pompous urban existence. Recognizably, these are "no more than the shadowy phantoms of imagination, which, he well knew, would never be realized" (IV, 245-47).

When the news arrives that his father has died intestate and left him, as eldest son, in possession of his property and fortune, his imaginative dream can become a reality:

> This was a sum that even exceeded his expectation, and could not fail to entertain his fancy with the most agreeable ideas. He found himself immediately a man of vast consequence among his country neighbours, who visited him with compliments of congratulation, and treated him with such respect as would have effectually spoiled any young man of his disposition, who had not the same advantages of experience as he had already purchased at a very extravagant price. Thus shielded with caution, he bore his prosperity with surprising temperance; everybody was charmed with his affability and moderation. (IV, 263)

With even Crabtree "almost reconciled to that institution, against which he had declaimed during the best part of his life," Peregrine joins with Emilia in wedlock, announcing his intent "to withdraw in private from the sea-wit of his friend Hatchway, who would otherwise retard his bliss with unseasonable impediments, which, at present, he could not possibly bear" (IV, 274-75).

Since it is never the fertile fancy, but rather its excess which is antithetical to social virtues, the creative imagination, now coupled with moral judgment, is for the first time capable of an esthetic which is neither self- nor socially-destructive. If we contend, as has Professor Putney, that "the sum of the episodes in *Peregrine Pickle* is the plot which ends in Peregrine's renunciation of the world for the joys of a tranquil life with Emilia," and that "the love story . . . is the core of the novel's structure,"[18] then we effectually distort the meaning of *love* and the significance of the *world* as they have been developed throughout the vast bulk of the novel. Peregrine's passion for Emilia can be gratified only after judgment has curbed the excesses of the pleasure-seeking imagination. Only then can the fertile fancy flourish in a world where pleasures must be harmonious, gregarious, and moderate.

REFERENCES

1. Ernest M. Baker, *The History of the English Novel* (London, 1930), IV, 209, cursorily dismisses the novel as "a further instalment of the farcical adventures, practical jokes, and amorous escapades that formed the staple of Roderick's history ashore." With an analysis no less slight, and obviously paraphrasing Baker, Lewis M. Knapp, *Tobias Smollett* (Princeton, 1949), p. 318, calls the book an "extension and intensification" of *Roderick Random* with "endless episodes crammed with slapstick adventure, practical jokes, and dull amours." W. E. Henley, *The Works of Tobias Smollett* (New York, 1899), I, xxiv, also condemns *Peregrine Pickle* as "farce, and farce again, and farce almost to the end." The only extended analysis of the novel is offered by Rufus Putney in "The Plan of *Peregrine Pickle*," *PMLA*, LX (1945), 1051-65. Putney argues persuasively, using the prefaces to *Roderick Random* and *Ferdinand Count Fathom* in formulating Smollett's theory of the novel, that Peregrine's adventures are not a haphazard collection of farcical episodes, but rather a well-planned whole: a satirical novel, aimed at teaching a moral lesson by picturing the follies and vices of the age.

2. References to Addison are from Henry Morley's edition of *The Spectator* (London, 1891). References to Hazlitt are from P. P. Howe's Centenary Edition of *The Complete Works of William Hazlitt* (London, 1931), VI, 5-30, 115-17; XII, 44-55.

3. A. S. P. Woodhouse, "Romanticism and the History of Ideas," in *English Studies Today*, ed. C. L. Wrenn and G. Bullough (Oxford, 1951), pp. 1020-40.

4. The dominant role of Adam Smith in bridging the gap between Addison and the Romantics is argued by Walter Jackson Bate, "The Sympathetic Imagination in Eighteenth-Century English Criticism," *ELH*, XI (1945), 144-64; and by Earl R. Wasserman, "The Sympathetic Imagination in Eighteenth-Century Theories of Acting," *JEGP*, XLVI (1947), 264-72.

5. Adam Smith, *The Theory of Moral Sentiments* (London, 1861), pp. 3-14.

6. John Ogilvie, "An Essay on the Lyric Poetry of the Ancients," *Poems* (London, 1762), pp. iv ff.

7. Alexander Gerard, *An Essay on Taste* (London, 1774), pp. 1-2, 95 ff.

8. James Beattie, *Dissertations Moral and Critical* (London, 1783), pp. 146-47, 165-68.

9. Clarence DeWitt Thorpe, "Addison and Hutcheson on the Imagination," *ELH*, II (1935), 215-34.

10. Francis Hutcheson, *An Essay on the Nature and Conduct of the Passions and Affections* (London, 1730), pp. 88-89, 114, 123. *An Inquiry into the Original of Our Ideas of Beauty and Virtue* (London, 1725), pp. 12-13.

11. Allusions to Peregrine as a "genius," with creative and inventive faculties, appear with frequency throughout the text. See I, 73, 75, 76, 77, 82, 102, 107, 108, 116, 142, 144, etc.

12. John S. Farmer and W. E. Henley, ed. *Slang and its Analogues* (London, 1902), V, 188. The title of Smollett's novel is quoted as an example of this colloquial usage.

13. Tobias Smollett, *The Present State of All Nations* (London, 1768), II, 213.

14. Alexander Gerard, *An Essay on Genius* (London, 1774), p. 54. With correspondences in image and idea that could have emanated only from the Scottish group, Gerard offers a fitting commentary on Smollett's novel: "Though genius be properly a comprehensive, regular, and active imagination, yet it can never attain perfection, or exert itself successfully on any subject, except it be united with a sound and piercing judgment. The vigour of imagination carries it forward to invention; but understanding must always conduct it and regulate its motions. . . . A fine imagination left to itself, will break out into bold sallies and wild extravagance, and overleap the bounds of truth or probability: but when it is put under the management of sound judgment, it leads to solid and useful invention, without having its natural sprightliness in the least impaired" (p. 71).

15. William Edward Mead, *The Grand Tour in the Eighteenth Century* (Boston, 1914). Smollett observes in *The Present State of All Nations*, II, 213, that in England "persons of fashion, after having studied at the university, commonly travel for improvement."

16. Howard Swazey Buck, *A Study of Smollett, chiefly "Peregrine Pickle"* (New Haven, 1925), pp. 20 ff. See also Rufus D. Putney, "Smollett and Lady Vane's Memoirs," *PQ*, XXV (1946), 120-26.

17. Putney, "The Plan of *Peregrine Pickle*." Although Professor Putney concedes that Smollett's plan for this novel is didactic and aims at teaching a moral lesson, he overlooks the opposition between imagination and judgment, crucial to the ethical scheme, and therefore concludes that Smollett's inferiority is due, not to his careless form or his inability to distinguish villain from hero, but to his "intellectual and spiritual limitations as a satiric novelist." Putney therefore distinguishes between Smollett's plot and his theme, the love story and the Hogarthian satire, and argues that "the love story . . . is the core of the novel's structure," while "the portrayal of society rather than the problem of the individual constitutes the novelist's chief end." The love episodes are, of course, to be interpreted within the eighteenth-century context of passions and reason, and related to the associated theme of imagination and judgment, from which the social satire derives its larger meaning. Given this additional dimension, plot and theme work together for the same end within Smollett's "plan."

18. See note 17 above.

CHAPTER FOUR. *FERDINAND COUNT FATHOM:*

A Study in Art and Nature

1. EARLY in *The Adventures of Ferdinand Count Fathom,* Smollett poses an antithesis between *art* and *nature,* common to eighteenth-century thought and crucial to the novel's core:

> Fathom, by dint of his insinuating arts, made shift to pass upon the schoolmaster as a lad of quick parts, in despite of a natural inaptitude to retain his lessons, which all his industry could never overcome.
>
> (I, 26)

By developing these "insinuating arts" which disguise his "natural inaptitude," Fathom succeeds in passing before the world at large as a man of sensibility and learning. His success is only short-lived, but coincident with his downfall and ultimate penitence, a dual recognition takes place. Fathom himself is to recognize the excess of his arts; but simultaneously men of natural sensibility and learning come to recognize their own defect, their failure to distinguish art from nature which in a major sense is responsible for their own shortcomings.

True, the above quotation has been culled almost at random from several hundred possible references to the art-nature antithesis in *Ferdinand Count Fathom.* Wrested out of its larger context, it provides, at best, a rather distorted picture of what *art* is and what *nature* is within the larger matrix which Smollett creates. Similar references can be extracted from much of eighteenth-century writing, where the antithesis is apparent in learned as well as popular texts. Hume insists in *A Treatise of Human Nature* that jus-

tice is "an artificial and not a natural virtue" (II, i, x), cognizant
that "when I deny justice to be a natural virtue, I make use of the
word, *natural,* only as oppos'd to *artificial*" (III, ii, i). Locke makes
a similar distinction in *An Essay Concerning Human Understanding,* where he notes that "in the species of artificial things,
there is generally less confusion and uncertainty than in natural,"
because artificial things are produced by men, whereas "in things
natural . . . differences and operations depend upon contriv-
ances beyond the reach of our discoveries" (III, 6, 40). The same
opposition is apparent in *The Microscope Made Easy,* where Henry
Baker observes that "an exceeding small *Needle* being . . . examined [under a microscope], the Point thereof appeared . . .
irregular, and unequal. . . . But the *Sting of a Bee* viewed
through the same Instrument, shewed every where a Polish most
amazingly beautiful, without the least Flaw, Blemish, or In-
equality." When comparing some Brussel's lace or some fine lawn
with a silkworm's web, the same distinction between art and nature
is drawn. "Thus sink the *Works of Art* when we become enabled
to see what they really are!—But, on the contrary, the nearer we
examine, the plainer we distinguish, the more we can discover of the
Works of Nature, . . ." Baker concludes (LI).

Popular writings reflect this same opposition. In the opening
of James Miller's play, *Art and Nature,* Truemore remarks about a
native whom he has brought back from the West Indies, "I shall
take great Pleasure in seeing pure simple Nature in him oppos'd to
Laws, Arts and Sciences amongst us." By the close of the drama the
Indian himself has announced, "Let us hear no more of your Laws,
your Arts, or your Sciences, for they are good for nothing. . . .
Let us go, and enjoy ourselves, and be as happy as Nature and
Common-Sense can make us." Fielding assumes the same kind of
opposition, when in *Tom Jones* he writes of Sophia's aunt:

> She perfectly well knew, though she had never practised them, all
> the arts which fine ladies use when they desire to give encourage-
> ment, or to conceal liking. . . . No species of disguise or affectation

had escaped her notice; but as to the plain simple workings of honest nature, as she had never seen any such, she could know but little of them. (VI, ii)

In John Moore's *Zeluco*, the hero's mother is "persuaded that nature had done so much for her son, that there was no need of the ornaments of art" (II). And Henry Mackenzie's introduction to *The Man of Feeling* describes Harley's manuscript in terms of the typical opposition as "a bundle of little episodes, put together without art, and of no importance on the whole, with something of nature, and little else in them."

Arthur O. Lovejoy's analysis of the diversity of meaning attached to the term *nature* describes the confusion current with most critics and historians. Like all great catchwords of history, *nature*—the most persistent, pervasive, and potent—is equivocal, or even multivocal, Professor Lovejoy explains. Though the word is one, the ideas it expresses are prodigiously multiple, varied, and frequently contradictory.[1] Nevertheless, the notion of an inherent opposition between *art* and *nature* still forms the standard academic formula for eighteenth-century studies.

One typical study, culling multiple references to the *art-nature* controversy from English verse written between 1725 and 1750, vividly sketches a poetic and horticultural "battleground," involving frequent "skirmishes" in which lovers of art and regularity championed rule-bound literature and sculptured hedgerows, while lovers of nature and diversity extolled uninhibited genius and irregular landscapes. This "warfare" ended in defeat for poets and gardeners who "continued to praise art's improvements on Nature's extravagance," and in victory for those who championed "the beautiful wildness of nature without the elegancies of Art."[2]

A similar struggle among critics of the age has been observed by Ronald S. Crane. Addison had distinguished two classes of geniuses, those formed by the rules, who "submitted the greatness of their natural talents to the corrections and restraints of art," and those who succeeded "by the mere strength of natural parts, and without any assistance of art or learning." We learn that "the opposition of the two types continued to be a favorite topic throughout the century," with later writers not hesitating "to assert the necessary precedence of the 'natural genius' over the genius formed by art and imitation."[3]

Basil Willey, who describes the century as a conflict between opposing forces of art and nature, observes that "both in England and France, there had been a succession of novels, plays, poems, and treatises exalting the natural over the artificial man, the primitive (as being the fresher from the hands of God or Nature) over the sophisticated, the rustic over the urban." Listed among those advocating the "natural man" are Addison, Thomson, Rousseau, Shaftesbury.[4]

This approach to an embattled eighteenth century is certainly not a recent one. A half-century ago Sir Leslie Stephen had interpreted the "return to nature" as a "revolutionary" movement which allowed the expression of emotions repressed by prior conventions. This "great revolution" gradually overthrew "the artificiality attributed to the eighteenth century," which had been "content to regulate their thoughts and lives by rules not traceable to first principles." As a result, "the revolt against it took again the form of an appeal to nature. Obviously nature was used in different and almost opposite senses. Wordsworth seemed to himself to be the antithesis to Pope, and yet Pope, like Wordsworth, preaches in one sense a worship of nature."[5]

This whole concept of "the romantic revolt," with an eventual supremacy of nature over artifice, of genius' fire over the restraining rules, of irregularity over uniformity, of originality over imitation, forms almost the standard approach to eighteenth-century studies. It is certainly discernible in Wordsworth's distinction between the natural poetry he and Coleridge were writing and the artificiality in which Pope had indulged.[6] Similarly, it can be adduced from the writings of Joseph and Thomas Warton, from Richard Hurd, and from works as early as Swift's *The Battle of the Books*. The opposition between *nature* and *art* was certainly a commonplace for the eighteenth-century mind. Unfortunately, for all its distance and perspective, the twentieth century still understands this opposition as an irreconcilable contradiction, an intellectual dilemma, an ideological dichotomy that could be resolved only by an ideological revolution. Oppositions, however, are not necessarily irreconcilable, and conflicts not always final dichotomies.

If we approach Smollett with no assumptions other than those afforded by the matrix of the novel, then the reconciliations he poses, like those offered by the Scottish Common-Sense writers, can be seen as bridging the gap between these hostile forces. Much of the same *pax in bello* which Smollett offers in *Ferdinand Count Fathom* is perceptible in *An Essay on the History of Civil Society*, where Adam Ferguson discerns that "art is natural to man; and . . . the skill he acquires after many ages of practice, is only the improvement of a talent he possessed at the first." True, "we speak of art as distinguished from nature; but art itself is natural to man," Ferguson explains. "He is in some measure the artificer of his own frame, as well as of his fortune, and is destined, from the first age of his being, to invent and contrive." Though we may see the *natural* as opposed to the *unnatural* in examining man's nature, these words "serve to distinguish nothing: for all the actions of man are equally the result of their nature."

> But if nature is only opposed to art, in what situation of the human race are the footsteps of art unknown? In the condition of the savage, as well as in that of the citizen, are many proofs of human invention; and in either is not any permanent station, but a mere stage through which this travelling being is destined to pass. If the palace be unnatural, the cottage is no less; and the highest refinements of political and moral apprehension, are not more artificial in their kind, than the first operations of sentiment and reason.
>
> If we admit that man is susceptible of improvement, and has in himself a principle of progression, and a desire of perfection, it appears improper to say, that he has quitted the state of his nature, when he has begun to proceed . . . . [for] like other animals, he only follows the disposition, and employs the powers that nature has given.
>
> The latest efforts of human invention are but a continuation of

certain devices which were practised in the earliest ages of the world, and in the rudest state of mankind.

As a result, Ferguson traces man's progress, not from a state of nature to a state of art, but from a state of rude art to a state of polished art.[7]

James Beattie makes almost the same assumptions about the naturalness of artifice. "Before the institution of government, men would live in what is called the state of nature, perfectly independent, equal, and free," Beattie writes in his *Moral Philosophy*.

> Though we here set government in opposition to the natural state, we must not call the former *unnatural: artificial* is the epithet which it derives from the contrast. Man is born naked; but clothes, though artificial, are not unnatural. Government, being an art useful to man, and indeed necessary to civilized man, must be agreeable to the intention of Providence, who made man what he is. . . .[8]

This same distinction between nature and an art which is artificial without being unnatural is drawn in his *Essay on Poetry and Musick*, where Beattie observes that good style is *"natural*, in contradistinction, not to *artificial* (itself being artificial) but to unnatural. . . ."[9]

In his *Lectures on Rhetoric* Hugh Blair establishes the same distinction as Ferguson and Beattie. Art can be differentiated from nature without necessarily being opposed to it, Blair contends. The ancients may excel us in delicacy of feeling and the natural fire of genius, but moderns have the advantage with art—"natural philosophy, astronomy, chemistry, and other sciences that depend on an extensive knowledge and observations of facts." Man ought not to be considered the product of either nature or art, but rather of the two combined:

> If the strength of genius be on one side, it will go far, in works of taste at least, to counterbalance all the artificial improvements which can be made by greater knowledge and correctness. . . . Among the ancients, we find higher conceptions, greater simplicity, more original

> fancy. Among the moderns, sometimes more art and correctness, but
> feebler exertions of genius.

To achieve any degree of perfection, however, man must develop both qualities, for good taste "in its perfect state . . . is
undoubtedly the result both of nature and of art."[10]

   This necessity for unifying nature and art, feelings and principles, is echoed by Alexander Gerard in *An Essay on Taste*. Assuming an inherent relationship between the esthetic and the moral,
Gerard argues that "fine taste is neither wholly the gift of *nature*,
nor wholly the effect of *art*," but a composite of the two. Though
fineness of taste "derives its origin from certain powers natural to
the mind . . . these powers cannot attain their full perfection,
unless they be assisted by proper culture." To cultivate one's taste,
the moral guiding powers of judgment must be unified with the
powers of imagination and sensibility; otherwise, either art or nature
may prove excessive and detrimental.[11]

   Significantly, these same congruities offered by Ferguson and
Beattie, Blair and Gerard, are apparent in Smollett's *Ferdinand
Count Fathom*. Examined within the limiting framework of
Smollett's novel, the terms *art* and *nature* reveal the writer adhering
equally to both of the controversial camps. He is on the side of *art*,
no less than on the side of *nature*—just as the Scottish Common-
Sense School adhered to both sides, and as reconciliations were
similarly possible for a large group of writers, apparently influenced
by the Scottish group, or affected by the same intangible forces that
were at work in Scotland during the century.

2. THROUGHOUT the novel, Count Fathom is most frequently described in terms of *art*. He is called successively a man of
"art and ingenuity" (I, 102); an "artful politician" (II, 42); an
"artful traitor" (II, 72, 171); an "artful serpent" (II, 226); an
"artful incendiary" (II, 61); the "artful Fathom" (II, 248), etc.

Despite ineptitudes, he passes as a lad of understanding by means of his "insinuating arts." Caught cheating, he maintains his innocence through "artful and ambiguous answers." Deficient in studies, he is acknowledged a genius in "other more profitable arts." To seduce his benefactor's daughter, he summons "all his artifice and attraction to his aid," employing them "under the insidious cover of profound respect" (I, 26-32). He seduces Wilhelmina "artfully," while true motives are disguised, just as he seduces her stepmother "with all his art" (I, 66-72). The passions of Elinor are "artfully concentred and kindled up" (I, 198), so that she becomes a ready prey to his appetites; and with "great art and perseverance" he puts the passions of Celinda under his command (I, 227). Like Peregrine Pickle, Fathom is most frequently a "genius," a man of "talent," a master of "invention." Whereas Pickle's genius is potentially creative and socially oriented, for the main part a perverted expression of his satirical disposition, Fathom's is a craft or cunning, disguising his disposition, his selfish appetites and passions.

Fathom's arts, no less than his appetites, are products of nature. Though they are artificial, they are not unnatural; and by developing his craft, Fathom develops his nature, for he is "calculated by nature to dupe even the most cautious, and gratify his appetites" (I, 25). He is "naturally a genius self-taught, in point of sagacity and invention" (I, 36), and his role of the wily fox, ambushing the ignorant and unwary, is one "for which he found himself best qualified by nature and inclination" (I, 55). "Naturally complaisant" (I, 150), Fathom simply turns to account his innate skills, "those ingratiating qualifications he inherited from nature" (I, 84).

He is also a "politician" (I, 41, 51, 63, 95, 108, etc.)—a word that assumed pejorative connotations in England from the late sixteenth through the eighteenth centuries, probably as a result of the popular misinterpretation of Machiavelli. Reinforced by the political theories of Hobbes, the term came to suggest the crafty intriguer, the shrewd schemer. With Ratchcali, Fathom enters into "an offensive and defensive alliance" (I, 56); just as with Theresa, a maid in the home of his patron, he forms a compact, Ovidian, as well as Machiavellian. Fathom "was never deficient in his political capacity" (I, 111), Smollett concedes, and "had he been admitted as a pupil in any political academy, would have certainly become one of the ablest statesmen in Europe" (1, 36). His landing in England is compared with Caesar's arrival on the island, and Scipio's landing in Africa (I, 179). Appropriately couched in military terms, his first conquest in England is a fellow-passenger on the coach to London:

> He gradually proceeded in sapping from one degree of intimacy to another, until all the bulwarks of her chastity were undermined, and she submitted to his desire; not with the reluctance of a vanquished people, but with all the transports of a joyful city, that opens its gates to receive a darling prince returned from conquest. (I, 198)

Sir Walter Scott writes "that the detestable Fathom is a living and existing miscreant, at whom we shrink as if from the presence of an incarnate fiend." Others have followed Scott in calling him a "monster of turpitude" or "an unbelievable seducer, imposter, and Iago-like monster."[12] This attitude is certainly suggested by various characters within the text, who also see Fathom in a Satanic role. Wilhelmina, an early victim of Fathom's arts, believes that "her lover was no other than the devil himself"; and on one occasion she even mistakes him "for Satan in *propria persona*" (I, 71). Her drunken father calls to him, "Come forth, Satan" (I, 75), when Fathom lies concealed in true Boccaccio-fashion within a huge chest, during an assignation with Wilhelmina's stepmother. A cavalier who challenges him to a duel, duped by Fathom's arts into believing him a man of supernatural courage, also considers Fathom "as a devil incarnate" (I, 218). Celinda regards him as "surely something supernatural" (I, 222); and Renaldo, once he is enlightened as to the true nature of Fathom, exclaims almost in Miltonic terms that he has "nourished a serpent in my bosom . . . who hath . . . perhaps ruined the pattern of all earthly perfection" (II, 165):

> That artful serpent Fathom glided into our mutual confidence, abused our ears, poisoned our unsuspected faith, and effected that fatal breach, productive of all the misery and vexation which we have suffered, and which is now so happily expelled. (II, 226)

Renaldo's view of earthly perfection, however, is to be distinguished from Smollett's. The principles under which Fathom operates are noticeably derived more from Hobbes or Mandeville, than from Miltonic Satanism—although the seventeenth and eighteenth centuries made increasing identification between Hobbes and diabolism. Of Fathom at the age of twelve, Smollett writes:

> The sole study, or at least the chief aim of Ferdinand, was to make himself necessary and agreeable to those on whom his dependence was placed. His talent was in this particular suited to his inclination; he seemed to have inherited it from his mother's womb; and, without all doubt, would have raised upon it a most admirable superstructure of fortune and applause, had not it been inseparably yoked with a most insidious principle of self-love, that grew up with him from the cradle, and left no room in his heart for the least particle of social virtue. This last, however, he knew so well how to counterfeit, by means of a large share of ductility and dissimulation, that, surely, he was calculated by nature to dupe even the most cautious, and gratify his appetites, by levying contributions on all mankind. (I, 25)

By the time he is eighteen, Fathom has formed a major conviction

> that the sons of men preyed upon one another, and such was the end and condition of their being. Among the principal figures of life, he observed few or no characters that did not bear a strong analogy to the savage tyrants of the wood. One resembled a tiger in fury and rapaciousness; a second prowled about like an hungry wolf, seeking whom he might devour; a third acted the part of a jackal, in beating the bush for game to his voracious employer; and the fourth imitated the wily fox, in practising a thousand crafty ambuscades for the destruction of the ignorant and unwary. This last was the department of life for which he found himself best qualified by nature and inclination; and he accordingly resolved that his talent should not rust in his possession.

As a result, Fathom arrives at the Hobbesian principles which un-
derlie his art, "determined to fascinate the judgment, rather than
the eyes of his fellow-creatures, by a continual exercise of that gift
of deceiving, with which he knew himself endued to an unrivalled
degree"; but also, "to acquire unbounded influence with those who
might be subservient to his interest, by an assiduous application to
their prevailing passions" (I, 55).

Thus, in Fathom's intrigue with Wilhelmina, the gratification of his voluptuous passions is primarily a *modus vivendi*, "for the
principal aim of the intrigue was to make her necessary to his in-
terested views" (I, 66). Both she and her stepmother are debauched
in order to "convert his good fortune to the purposes of that principle, from which his view was never, no, not for a moment, detached" (I, 77). Fathom's arts are employed consistently according
to principle:

> His aim was to dwell among the tents of civil life . . . and render
> mankind subservient to his interest, not by stratagems which irritate,
> but by that suppleness of insinuation, which could not fail to soothe
> the temper of those on whom he meant to prey.   (I, 105)

This is the end behind Fathom's artifice, his guile and craft
and political astuteness. Here, in rendering "mankind subservient
to his interest," his true genius resides.

This inter-relationship between art and politics, genius and
self-love, principles and passions—all rising from Fathom's basic
nature—is not too remote from the state of nature Hobbes depicts
in his *Leviathan*, where "Nature (the Art whereby God hath made
and governes the World) is by the *Art* of man, as in many other
things, so in this also imitated, that it can make an Artificial Animal." This "Artificial Animal," as all readers of Hobbes recognize,
is the Commonwealth or State, formed because of "the characters
of mans heart, blotted and confounded as they are, with dissem-
bling, lying, counterfeiting, and erroneous doctrines." Because of
man's desire for gain, for safety and reputation, "the condition of
Man . . . is a condition of Warre of every one against every one,"

Hobbes explains. Governments and social contracts result from a
first law of nature, the search for peace; but there exists simultaneously a second law, "the summe of the Right of Nature; which is,
By all means we can, to defend our selves."[13]

3. OVERWHELMINGLY, critics of the eighteenth century
have neatly divided the period between adherents of Hobbes and
Mandeville who insisted on man's innate selfishness, and followers
of Shaftesbury and Hutcheson who argued theories of innate
benevolence and generosity.[14] Whereas Fathom is clearly an advo-
cate of Hobbesian principles, Smollett reveals an adherence to
neither Hobbesian nor Shaftesburian moral laws, but admits the
validity of both. In *Ferdinand Count Fathom*, commenting causti-
cally on Fathom's success, he projects a concept of nature in which
benevolence is "as universal, if not as natural," as selfishness:

> Success . . . would, by a disciple of Plato, and some modern moral-
> ists, be ascribed to the innate virtue and generosity of the human
> heart, which naturally espouses the cause that needs protection. But
> I, whose notions of human excellence are not quite so sublime, am
> apt to believe . . . that spirit of self-conceit and contradiction . . .
> is, at least, as universal, if not as natural, as the moral sense so warmly
> contended for by those ideal philosophers.   (II, 116-17)

Accordingly, since Fathom's antagonists in this *bellum omnium
contra omnes* include all of mankind, they fall into two definitive
groups.

First, there are the artful—Theresa and Ratchcali; Sir Giles
and Sir Stentor; the ostentatious jeweler, his envious wife and
daughter; Mr. and Mrs. Trapwell; Fathom's solicitor; and Maurice,
the valet. Like Fathom himself, they are adept at counterfeiting
virtue and generosity to hide their Hobbesian principles.

But there is also a second group, the artless, whose virtues and
sensibilities make them easy prey. Here, belong the Count de Mel-

vil, his son and daughter; Don Diego and his daughter, "Monimia"; Madame Clement; the Jew, Joshua; Major Farrel; Elinor and Celinda.

The young Count de Melvil, Fathom's chief antagonist, is most representative of this second group. Because Fathom shares in the education and amusements of his patron's son, an intimacy and friendship soon develop. "Yet their dispositions were altogether different, and their talents unalike," Smollett insists (I, 24). "He and the young Count formed a remarkable contrast, which, in the eye of the world, redounded to his advantage" (I, 54). Renaldo cultivates his studies and develops his understanding. For him these seem "of more real importance than the exteriors and forms of life," than the "bashful appearance and uncouth address" he exhibits. In contrast, Fathom, "who was in point of learning a mere dunce, became, even in childhood, remarkable among the ladies for his genteel deportment and vivacity"; therefore he cultivates his proficiency in dancing, in wit, and in *politesse* (I, 24-25).

> They were certainly, in all respects, the reverse of each other. Renaldo, under a total defect of exterior cultivation, possessed a most excellent understanding, with every virtue that dignifies the human heart; while the other, beneath a most agreeable outside . . . concealed an amazing fund of villany and ingratitude.   (I, 54)

Renaldo is a man "whose notions of honour were scrupulously rigid and romantic, whose temper was warm, and whose love was intense" (II, 33). Like his father, who is "naturally of a generous disposition" (I, 28), and like his sister, who too is imbued with "natural generosity" (I, 43), Renaldo constantly reveals "that warmth of sympathy and benevolence which was natural to his heart" (II, 183). He displays a rough and boorish exterior in his youth, but he possesses "a large share of generous sensibility" (I, 28) and a heart which has "never known the instigations of fraud" (II, 23).

Thus, Renaldo, who *appears* early as a boor, is in reality a man of understanding, virtue, and sensibility. Fathom, who *appears* to be understanding, virtuous, and a man of sensibility, is in reality an ungracious villain. Through his natural *art*, Fathom manages to conceal his artful *nature* from "the eye of the world," that external vision which mistakes appearances for reality, art for nature, superficial polish for enlightenment, selfishness for sensibility. Once "the eye" is replaced by understanding, the outer vision by real insights, the downfall of Fathom becomes imminent.

For Fathom *nature* is a craft or skill, closely allied with the political, an adeptness in concealing his real disposition, his lack of sensibility, his passions, his selfishness, artifice and materialism. For young Count de Melvil *nature* is identified with the heart, with sensibility, with benevolence, sentiment and understanding.

Other characters within this *artless* group certainly display qualities which parallel those of Renaldo. Monimia, whom Renaldo eventually marries, is consistently a paragon of virtue, "mistress of every elegant qualification, natural and acquired" (I, 163), "by nature fraught with that sensibility which refines the sentiment and taste." Madame Clement, who rescues her from Fathom, reveals a "frankness which is the result of true benevolence," as well as eyes which are constantly "bedewed with the drops of sympathy and compassion" (II, 80-82). Artlessness is also integral to Major Farrel and to the "benevolent Israelite," both devoted to Renaldo's cause. Don Diego, too, reveals himself as a man of natural feeling, frequently giving way to tears, and alternating between transports of grief, joy, and fury. Celinda is pictured as "an artless innocent young creature" with a "sensibility . . . diffused through all the passions of her heart" (I, 221-28). Similarly, Elinor is "an innocent unsuspecting country damsel" (I, 194), debauched by Fathom, but with sufficient compassion to marry him later when he is impoverished and penitent.

Fathom's state of war against all mankind necessarily involves another group: those who, like him, are artful counterfeiters of natural sensibility and benevolence, disguising their real selfish motives.

He forms political alliances with some, but these are recognizably temporary expediencies which frequently redound to his disadvantage. He finds a ready accomplice in Theresa, already master of "little arts, by which a woman strives to . . . ensnare the heart of a man" (I, 35); and through his artful instructions, she aids in pressing his suit for her mistress, Mademoiselle de Melvil. On several occasions Fathom enters into alliances with Ratchcali, the Tyrolese (I, 56, 200). These serve his ends temporarily, but on both occasions the Tyrolese proves the superior artist and absconds with Fathom's wealth, aided the second time by his crafty valet and by Fathom's artful solicitor.

Fathom also pits his art against the "reciprocal envy and malevolence" (I, 61) of Wilhelmina and the jeweler's wife; and despite some narrow escapes, he is ultimately victorious. It is far different when his skill is pitted against the wiles of Sir Stentor, disguised as a gullible English country booby while secretly allied with Sir Giles. Here, Fathom is "fairly foiled at his own weapons" (I, 148). And it is different with Mrs. Trapwell, "void of any principle, and extremely addicted to pleasure" (I, 236), for she arranges with her crafty spouse to discover her and Fathom together during an assignation.

When Fathom's art is concentrated upon the artful and unprincipled, the effect is generally comic or satiric, for the conflict emerges as a battle of art against art, wit against wit. Since compassion has been precluded for either the protagonist or his crafty antagonists by their very natures, one tends less to sympathize with the victims of these petty intrigues, and more to admire the skill and wit of the victor.

However, when Fathom pits his cunning against the artless and natural, with whom sympathies have obviously been aligned, results border on the sentimental and tragic. This split in tone accounts in part, undoubtedly, for the not infrequent observation that the novel as a whole fails to sustain an artistically unified impression, beginning as it does with a cynical note, which prepares the reader inadequately for the sentimental ending.[15] Yet this tonal bifurcation cannot account entirely for disunity in *Ferdinand Count Fathom*, for Sterne's *Sentimental Journey* is highly successful with its admixture of pathos and mirth. Unfortunately, in Smollett's novel, tonal disunity is reinforced by a weakness in architectonics.

4. DIVISIBLE into four major parts, *Ferdinand Count Fathom* offers not only two distinct climaxes, one for each of the two middle sections, but also a new protagonist for the final section. These factors seriously impede the development of form; however, at the same time they reveal much of an insight into Smollett's purposes with the novel.

The initial section (chs. I-X), concerned with Fathom's birth and early training, is instrumental in determining the role he is to adopt later in the novel, for Fathom's art is both natural and learned. Born, as he was to live, in the midst of war, he owes allegiances to no particular society, "for, though he first saw the light in Holland, he was not born till after the carriage arrived in Flanders." His family ties are almost as minimal:

> that he was acknowledged by no mortal sire, solely proceeded from the uncertainty of his mother, whose affections were so dissipated among a number of admirers, that she could never pitch upon the person from whose loins our hero sprung.

His nursery is among the Austrian Army, where his artistic mother proves equally "adept in the art of stripping" the dead and making "artful declaration[s]" in flattering the living. His milk is the wine his mother dispenses among the military, for she is "resolved to improve upon the ordinances of nature, and foster him with a juice much more energetic than the milk of goat, wolf, or woman." Before he is thirteen months old, he is taught "to suck brandy impregnated with gunpowder, through the touchhole of a pistol." At six, young Ferdinand is conducted to the frontiers of the Turkish-Austrian war, which his mother considered "the most consummate school of life, and proposed for the scene of his instruction." By the time he is nine, when his mother receives a brace of bullets in her brain, Fathom is unusually prepared for the more general battleground of civil society on which he is to practice his skills (I, 7-19).

He has already been equipped for entrance into the skirmishes of civil society by the time of his mother's death. "Being naturally of a generous disposition," and owing a debt to Fathom's mother who has saved his life, the Count de Melvil has already undertaken Fathom's education and admitted him into his tent as one of his domestics. Here, Fathom's artistic career begins. He suffers no sorrow at the loss of his mother, yet he has sufficient art to counterfeit appearances. As a result, the Count, a "man of extraordinary benevolence, looked upon the boy as a prodigy of natural affection." Before he is eighteen, Fathom has successfully ingratiated himself with the entire family, their friends, his tutor, as well as with the general domestic staff, which he dominates through Theresa (I, 21-28).

The second major section (chs. XI-XXXVIII) marks the beginning of a series of stages whereby Fathom, through successful application of his arts, achieves his ends—position, wealth, and affluence, which his low birth has denied him. Before, "his observation had been confined to a narrow sphere." Now, with age and experience "his perceptions began to be more distinct"; whereas "he had formerly imagined" the validity of his Hobbesian principles, he was "now fully persuaded" of their truth (I, 54). Moving consecutively from the Count's castle at Presburg to Vienna, then to the Army, Paris, and finally to England, he mounts to the height of his career, posing as gentleman, connoisseur, and learned physician:

> The most superficial tincture of the arts and sciences in such a juggler, is sufficient to dazzle the understanding of half mankind; and, if managed with circumspection, will enable him to spend his life among the literati, without once forfeiting the character of a connoisseur.
>
> Our hero was perfectly master of this legerdemain. . . .

Nothing was so wretched among the productions of art, that he could not impose upon the world as a capital performance; and so fascinated were the eyes of his admirers, he could easily have persuaded them that a barber's bason was an Etrurian patera, and the cover of a copper pot no other than the shield of Ancus Martius. In short, it was become so fashionable to consult the Count in everything relating to taste and politeness.   (I, 207, 211)

Aside from early forays among the de Melvils, which are minor and directed only toward material ends, Fathom's first skirmishes are with the artful in society. His gains from the jeweler's family are lost to the crafty Ratchcali; the deficit is made up with the conniving old woman in the forest, but this also is lost, to the wiles of Sir Stentor and Sir Giles. Not until the middle of this second section does he commit an act of unmitigated evil, when he uses all his arts against Don Diego. From this point, his genius is indiscriminately pitted against the artless and artful alike, in his steady rise in English society. Eventually, he is trapped by the ingenious Mrs. Trapwell, gulled by his clever solicitor, fleeced by his valet Maurice, and betrayed yet another time by his accomplice Ratchcali. Then, "deprived of his reputation, rank, liberty, and friends; and his fortune reduced from two thousand pounds to something less than two hundred" (I, 253), he is carried off to jail.

The third major section (chs. XXXIX-LVI), beginning with Fathom in prison, traces his reascendence in society, once he is rescued by Renaldo. Both Renaldo and his love Monimia become major targets for Fathom's machinations. But again, his ascent is doomed. For a second time he faces a climactic fall, poverty and imprisonment—though now the situational reverse is accompanied by sorrow and penitence.

Already weakened by a tonal bifurcation, through rapid alternation of comic and tragic effects, the structure of the novel gains little by this second climax, which only parallels the rise and decline delineated in the prior section. Indubitably, action here provides little for plot movement that could not have been achieved readily by assimilating essential incidents within the development of section two. Although section three provides little for architectonics, it does provide emphasis, through reiteration, on the causes for Fathom's rise and fall.

The primal cause for Fathom's rise, his artfulness, has already been developed at length. But there exists a perceptible corollary to Fathom's artistic techniques. This is the obvious lack of art within the world of sensibility, its lack of skill in readily differentiating artifice from nature, and consequently its inability to cope with it. Thus, Count de Melvil is first deceived by the youthful Ferdinand, only because he mistakenly attributes to the boy, through his own prejudices, what he knows to be really in himself. *Because* he is "himself a man of extraordinary benevolence" (I, 21), he is blinded to the lack of virtue in others. The old Count is only one among "the ignorant and unwary," ensnared by Fathom, "the wily fox . . . practising a thousand crafty ambuscades" (I, 55). By the same token, the innocence of Celinda and Elinor, the unsuspecting nature of Renaldo, the perfect virtue of Monimia which admits no evil or deception, the unwariness of the world at large—all contribute to Fathom's phenomenal rise to success. As Mademoiselle de Melvil counsels her brother, "Nothing is more easy . . . than to impose upon a person, who, being himself unconscious of guile, suspects no deceit. You have been a dupe, dear brother, not to the finesse of Fathom, but to the sincerity of your own heart" (II, 162).

In this light we must read the crucial opening chapter which refutes Cardinal de Retz's theory that, the truest history being derived from autobiographical statements, men of importance (provided they have enough honesty) ought to write their own memoirs. To this, the common-sense Smollett replies that honesty and objectivity are rarities: "Indeed, I will venture to say, that, how upright soever a man's intentions may be, he will . . . be sometimes misled by his own phantasy, and represent objects, as they appeared to him, through the mists of prejudice and passion." Fittingly, he himself assumes the task of writing the adventures of Fathom, certain that "by the time the reader shall have glanced over the subsequent sheets, I doubt not but that he will bless God that the adventurer was not his own historian." Again, significantly at the opening of his preface, Smollett writes of the "passions, which frequently warp the opinion, and perplex the understanding of the most judicious." Between all the passions agitating the human mind, "there is an affinity and short transition," he later explains, but "they are all false perspectives, which, though they magnify, yet perplex and render indistinct every object which they represent. And flattery is never so successfully administered, as to those who know they stand in need of friendship, assent, and approbation" (I, 197).

The impassioned sincerity of Renaldo's own heart, then, contributes to the rise of Fathom. Excessive feelings, a prejudice for sensibility, must be overcome, before Renaldo and those like him can avoid those "false perspectives" which confuse art with nature, appearance with reality.

These are the forces then which contribute to the rise of Fathom. But pervasive forces also contribute to his decline. Before the end of the second section, and again before the close of the third, these successfully coalesce in bringing about Fathom's downfall.

Foremost among these is the excessiveness of Fathom's appetites, an intemperance which counteracts his craft, for "Fathom, with all his circumspection, had a weak side, which exposed him to sundry mischances; this was his covetousness, which on some occasions became too hard for his discretion" (I, 240). Indeed, Smollett notes, Fathom's genius might have raised both fortune and applause "had not it been inseparably yoked with a most insidious principle of self-love"(I, 25). This is "an infirmity of his constitution, which he could not overcome" (II, 127), and which "all his philosophy and caution could hardly keep within bounds" (II, 118).

> There was an intemperance in his blood, which often interfered with his caution; and although he had found means to render this heat sometimes subservient to his interest, yet, in all probability, Heaven

mingled the ingredient in his constitution, on purpose to counteract his consummate craft, defeat the villany of his intention, and at least expose him to the justice of the law, and the contempt of his fellow-creatures. (II, 29-30)

Fathom's appetites are excessive, but concomitantly, his arts which conceal them frequently prove insufficient—before the world of sensibility and artlessness, but also before the world of art.

They are insufficient before the world of art. His first decline is a consequence of insufficiency before the cumulative arts of the Trapwells, Ratchcali, Maurice, and his solicitor. His second decline results from an insufficiency before the artful advances of Miss Biddy and her mother; an inadequacy in dealing with the clergyman's wife, whose chastity he mastered, though without quieting her conscience; deficiencies with the widow, Sarah Muddy, whom he marries for a nonexistent fortune; and shortcomings with the clever empiric, Doctor Buffalo. Only at this point, at the lowest ebb of his career, does Fathom achieve a belated recognition:

> Such a concurrence of sinister events made a deep impression upon the mind of our adventurer. All his fortitude was insufficient to bear him up against this torrent of misfortunes; his resources were all dried up, his invention failed, and his reflection began to take a new turn. . . .
>
> These reflections, which, perhaps, the misery of his fellow-creatures would never have inspired, had he himself remained without the verge of misfortune, were now produced from the sensation of his own calamities; and, for the first time, his cheeks were bedewed with the drops of penitence and sorrow. . . .
>
> Be that as it may, he certainly, after a tedious and fruitless exercise of his invention, resolved to effect a clandestine retreat from that confederacy of enemies which he could not withstand, and once more join his fortune to that of Renaldo, whom he proposed to serve, for the future, with fidelity and affection, thereby endeavouring to atone for the treachery of his former conduct. (II, 139-41)

Before he can properly atone for his treachery, however, Fathom is seized and imprisoned.

Fathom's arts also prove insufficient before the natural world, although this does not become evident until the fourth section, when with all abruptness Fathom is abandoned as protagonist, and Renaldo substituted in his place.

Section four (chs. LVII-LXVII) shifts to the point of view of Renaldo, who comes increasingly, though belatedly, to recognize "the perfidy of mankind" (II, 182) in general, and of Fathom in particular. Returning to Hungary, accompanied by the compassionate Major Farrel, Renaldo quickly frees his family and fortune from the perfidious Count Trebasi. There, through his sister, he suddenly learns of Theresa's confession to her base alliance with Fathom; and through his sister also, he learns of her chance meeting with Wilhelmina, now a nun, and of Fathom's iniquities with the jeweler and his family. A letter from Monimia enlightens him further about the perfidious Fathom. Hastening to England to rejoin Monimia, Renaldo meets with a contrite Ratchcali and later with Don Diego, who offer further evidence of Fathom's arts. Thus, it is an enlightened Nature that reigns supreme by the close of the novel, when Monimia is reunited with Renaldo, and also with her father, Don Diego.

Like the bifurcation in tone already noted, and like the duplication of plot lines within the middle sections, this substitution of Renaldo as protagonist in this final section of the novel considerably weakens the architectonics. As Smollett explains in his preface, however, the primary end of the noval is ethical and didactic:

> That the mind might not be fatigued, nor the imagination disgusted, by a succession of vicious objects, I have endeavoured to refresh the attention with occasional incidents of a different nature; and raised up a virtuous character, in opposition to the adventurer, with a view to amuse the fancy, engage the affection, and form a striking contrast which might heighten the expression, and give a *relief* to the moral of the whole.

In rather precise terms, Smollett elaborates upon this "moral of the whole." His intentions, as outlined in the preface, are "to

unfold the mysteries of fraud, to instruct the ignorant, and entertain the vacant," to provide

> a beacon for the benefit of the unexperienced and unwary, who, from
> the perusal of these memoirs, may learn to avoid the manifold snares
> with which they are continually surrounded in the paths of life; while
> those who hesitate on the brink of iniquity may be terrified from
> plunging into that irremediable gulf, by surveying the deplorable fate
> of *Ferdinand Count Fathom.*

In his use of terror, Smollett is proposing an esthetic obviously derived from Addison's *Pleasures of the Imagination* and reaching its
greatest expression in Edmund Burke, for whom terror was the
greatest source of the sublime. For Smollett, as for Addison and
Burke, "the impulses of fear, which is the most violent and interest-
ing of all the passions, remain longer than any other upon the
memory." In this way, Smollett justifies his use of Fathom, in preference to Renaldo, as the major material of his novel:

> such monsters ought to be exhibited to public view, that mankind
> may be upon their guard against imposture; that the world may see
> how fraud is apt to overshoot itself; and that, as virtue, though it may
> suffer for a while, will triumph in the end; so iniquity, though it may
> prosper for a season, will at last be overtaken by that punishment and
> disgrace which are its due.   (II, 87)

While the use of Renaldo as major protagonist might have
provided the novel with a unity lacking in its present form, this
would have had dire consequences. First, it would have necessitated
abandonment of terror as the manner for provoking Smollett's
didactic ends. But also, it would have resulted in a form and purpose
almost identical with that of *Roderick Random*. Clearly, Smollett
was here creating a counterpart to his first novel. That he recognized the inadequacy of plot, as embodied in Fathom, to bring about
intended goals is perhaps best attested by his ultimate shift to
Renaldo as hero.

Coleridge has commented that the novel, like *Volpone* and

Zeluco, is "a tale in which there is no goodness of heart in any of
the prominent characters."[16] Such criticism can emanate only from
a complete disregard for Smollett's professed ends, as from a disregard for the eighteenth-century framework of *art* and *nature* against
which Fathom has been so carefully placed. Fathom represents not
the inexorable villain, lacking in "goodness of heart," but rather the
excessiveness of *art,* operating with only a certain degree of approbation within a blinded world of *nature.* Only if our own Shaftesburian sensibilities accept the world as Eden, Monimia as heavenly
perfection, Renaldo as a disillusioned Adam—a picture which Smollett consistently satirizes and ultimately rejects—only then can
Fathom be interpreted as a serpent in Paradise.

When the novelist abandons Fathom as major protagonist, the
structure is considerably weakened. But with Smollett, as always,
architectonics are not primary. His major concern is neither with the
triumph of nature nor with the downfall of art. Clearly, he is more
concerned with a common-sense *rapprochement* of the two opposing ideologies. Resultant is a conclusion in which excessive *art* is
encouraged to put its talents to better use in civil society, and defec-
tive *nature* is taught to moderate its excessive sensibility.

This is certainly a conclusion for which there has been ade-
quate preparation throughout, for Fathom's arts represent an extension of and development from nature. As a result, artifice becomes
natural, and artificiality is to be distinguished only from the unnatural. Fathom's arts not only are natural, but are cultivated and
developed by his genius and talents, with implications that are
moral, as well as esthetic. In addition, both art and nature are held
up as virtues in a state of moderation. Thus, Fathom's art is undeniably advantageous in dealing with the artful; with them, he is
frequently deficient rather than excessive in his craft. In addition,
his selfish passions, which are disguised by his arts, are condemned
only for their excess, which Fathom must eventually learn to control. Renaldo too has natural appetites and passions, and although
these are socially and not selfishly oriented, in their excessive state
they are responsible for prejudices and false perspectives which

distort the understanding. Renaldo's natural passions and feelings are undoubtedly both advantageous and virtuous in dealing with the natural. But in dealing with the artful they are excessive and impede fulfillment of his own goals.

REFERENCES

1. Arthur O. Lovejoy, *Essays in the History of Ideas* (Baltimore, 1948), pp. xii-xiii, 69-77.

2. Margaret Fitzgerald, *First Follow Nature* (New York, 1947), pp. 127 ff.

3. Ronald S. Crane, "English Criticism: Neo-Classical," in *Dictionary of World Literature,* ed. Joseph T. Shipley (New York, 1943), pp. 193 ff.

4. Basil Willey, *The Eighteenth Century Background* (London, 1950), pp. 240-41.

5. Leslie Stephen, *History of English Thought* (New York, 1881), II, 447-48.

6. The distinction is central to the whole of *The Prelude,* though it is stated most boldly in the preface to the *Lyrical Ballads,* where Wordsworth announces his intention of tracing through "the primary laws of our nature" in his use of "humble and rustic life." His admonition, "that there is no necessity to trick out or to elevate nature," is in decided opposition to Pope's lines, "True Wit is Nature to advantage dressed, / What oft was thought, but ne'er so well expressed." Coleridge contends in *Biographia Literaria* (ch. XVII) that Wordsworth's preface was urging "a reformation in our poetic diction," one which would strip it of the "mere artifices of connection or ornament" and induce a "natural language of impassioned feeling."

7. Adam Ferguson, *An Essay on the History of Civil Society* (London, 1773), pp. 10-15, 280.

8. James Beattie, *Moral Philosophy* (Philadelphia, 1809), III, 4-7.

9. James Beattie, *Essays* (Philadelphia, 1809), III, 3-5, 25.

10. Hugh Blair, *Lectures on Rhetoric* (Philadelphia, 1846), pp. 20-21, 390-91.

11. Alexander Gerard, *An Essay on Taste* (Edinburgh, 1790), pp. 1, 83-103.

12. Walter Scott, *Lives of Eminent Novelists and Dramatists* (London, n.d.), p. 465. Ernest Baker, *The History of the English Novel* (London, 1930), IV, 217. Lewis M. Knapp, *Tobias Smollett* (Princeton, 1949), p. 319.

13. Thomas Hobbes, *Leviathan* (New York, 1950), pp. 3-5, 101-07.

14. *Infra*, ch. V.

15. Knapp, p. 320. Baker, p. 216.

16. Samuel T. Coleridge, *Miscellaneous Criticism*, ed. Thomas Middleton Raysor (Cambridge, Mass., 1936), p. 55.

CHAPTER FIVE. *SIR LAUNCELOT GREAVES:*

A *Study in Social- and Self-Love*

1. *The Adventures of Sir Launcelot Greaves* first made its appearance in monthly installments of the *British Magazine* between January, 1760, and December, 1761. During this same time, Smollett seems to have been working on his translation of *Don Quixote*, first issued in 1755 and published in a second corrected edition in 1761.

Obvious parallels between Smollett's and Cervantes' hero appear to have determined the direction for criticism during the next two centuries. Following Sir Walter Scott, who contended that Sir Launcelot's knight-errantry is assumed only that it "may make him the more exact counterpart to the Knight of La Mancha," critics have almost unanimously dismissed the eighteenth-century work as an inferior imitation.[1] Since Smollett's protagonist is referred to within the text as "a modern Don Quixote," readers have not been without internal evidence for this view. Yet, Sir Launcelot's refutation of this charge has generally been overlooked:

> I am neither an affected imitator of Don Quixote, nor, as I trust in Heaven, visited by that spirit of lunacy so admirably displayed in the fictitious character exhibited by the inimitable Cervantes. I have not yet encountered a windmill for a giant, nor mistaken this public-house for a magnificent castle. . . . (p. 16)

James Beattie is one of the few to detect major differences between Sir Launcelot and his sixteenth-century predecessor. A Scottish contemporary of Smollett, Beattie admits great merit for the eighteenth-century work and finds it "truly original in the execution, notwithstanding that the hint is borrowed from Don Quixote." Insistent that "Sir Launcelot Greaves is of Don Quixote's kindred, but a different character," he explains that Smollett's design is "not to expose him to ridicule, but rather to recommend him to our pity and admiration."[2]

Close examination of basic motifs in Smollett sustains Beattie's view that similarities between Launcelot and Quixote are only superficial. Smollett has translated Cervantes' device into his own contemporary terms, so that the novel emerges as a reflection of the typical eighteenth-century controversy between social- and self-love. From the beginning Launcelot is a man of "extravagant benevolence," whose "generosity seemed to overleap the bounds of discretion and even in some cases might be thought tending to a breach of the king's peace" (p. 53). As an eighteenth-century knight, Sir Launcelot has "declared perpetual war" against "the foes of virtue and decorum" (p. 16). Though we admire his social virtues, at the same time we pity his extravagance—as Beattie is quick to discern— for coupled with the extravagance is a madness which almost prevents the fulfillment of a self-interest, his passion for Aurelia Darnel. Before the close of the novel, Sir Launcelot is forced to recognize his own excesses and to abandon the chivalric role, content to exercise a more limited social good, in order that he might effect a consummation of self-interests.

This basic theme, the controversy surrounding social- and self-love, has long been regarded as a commonplace in eighteenth-century thought. Sir Leslie Stephen called this a problem around which "raged the most active controversies of the period" and recognized that "the typical representatives of the two schools of thought in the early part of the century were Shaftesbury and Mandeville, both of them writers of remarkable ability and of great influence upon their contemporaries and successors."[3] For Shaftesbury, who believed that man was essentially altruistic and gregarious, the coincidence of private and public good was a result of enlightened benevolence; but Mandeville, convinced of the inherent egoism of all men, insisted public good was merely a consequence of self-interests. Mandeville himself pointed to his divergences from Shaftesbury, when he insisted belligerently in *The Fable of the Bees*, at the opening of the section entitled "A Search into the Nature of Society," that "two Systems cannot be more opposite than his Lordship's and mine." Although Mandeville did not begin any systematic attack on Shaftesbury until his 1723 edition, he succeeded then in launching a full-scale attack upon the author of the *Characteristics* that was to reverberate throughout the century.[4]

Of course this controversy did not begin with Mandeville, but had its immediate antecedents in the seventeenth century, when the Cambridge Platonists were quarreling with Hobbes over the same problems. Countering Hobbes's contention that good was merely that which every man desired, the Platonists were insistent on the universality of a "Boniform Faculty of the Soul," an inner sense which provided all men with an objective and intuitive standard for ethical judgment. Manifestations of this seventeenth-century conflict are clearly discernible in the sixteenth-century Epicureans, in some of the extreme followers of Duns Scotus in the thirteenth century, and, of course, in the Greek sophists.[5]

Regardless of when the beginnings of this opposition occurred, cultural historians are almost unanimous in discerning its climactic state in eighteenth-century thought. Manifestations appear in works of a most diverse nature. Edmund Burke, considering the social passions in *On the Sublime and Beautiful*, assumes that "absolute and entire *solitude*, that is, the total and perpetual exclusion from all society, is as great a positive pain as can almost be conceived" (I, xi). William Cowper observes in "Charity" that "God, working ever on a social plan, / By various ties attaches man to man" (ll. 15-16). In Fielding's *Amelia*, terms of the conflict are obvious when the heroine cries, "Sure all mankind almost are villains in their hearts"; and she is soundly rebuked by Doctor Harrison, who launches into a typical discussion of man's ethical nature: "The nature of man is far from being in itself evil; it abounds with benevolence, charity, and pity, coveting praise and honour, and shunning shame and disgrace. Bad education, bad habits, and bad customs, debauch our nature, and drive it headlong as it were into vice" (IX, v).

Many of the thinkers and writers of the period fell into either of the two extremes and were categorized as ardent believers in man's natural benevolence or as staunch advocates of man's natural selfishness. Yet, there was a considerable number who insisted on a common-sense middle ground and who reconciled what for much of the century was a major ethical contradiction. For example, Squire Allworthy in Fielding's *Tom Jones* eventually learns that his excessive benevolence has allowed him to be taken in by appearances and to reward Blifil mistakenly as the generous one, while chastising Tom as the selfish villain. As Blifil finally reminds him, "Compassion for those who do not deserve it, I own is a crime; and yet it is a crime from which you yourself are not entirely free" (XVIII, v). Precisely the same kind of development is apparent in Goldsmith's *Vicar of Wakefield*, where Doctor Primrose comes to realize that excessive benevolence, having colored his understanding, has led to many woes—to a condemnation of the generous "Mr. Burchell" and to praise of the egoistic traitor, Mr. Thornhill. Like Burchell, who himself "carried benevolence to an excess when young . . . so that he began to lose a regard for private interest in universal sympathy" (III), the good Doctor achieves a belated recognition of the inadequacies of his Shaftesburian philosophy. Alexander Pope, too, argues a common-sense approach to the two seemingly antithetical doctrines in *An Essay on Man,* where the prose preface notes his aim of "steering betwixt the extremes of doctrines seemingly opposite." It is only through self-knowledge, Pope insists throughout the second Book, that man can see the larger harmony of the universe, the general frame linked by God and Nature, so that "Self-Love and Social are the same." The antidote to excess becomes "Know then thyself," as the only means of reconciling feelings with the understanding, altruism with egotism, for "Reason, Passion, answer one great aim," and "True Self-Love and Social are the same."

The largest and most obvious group of writers concerned with the reconciliation of these contraries, was, of course, the Scottish Common-Sense School. Beginning with Francis Hutcheson, the Scottish group was almost unanimous in its attempt to reconcile Hobbes and Mandeville with Shaftesbury. "As all Men have *Self-Love*, as well as *Benevolence*," Hutcheson had insisted, "these two Principles may jointly excite a Man to the same Action; and then they are to be consider'd as two Forces impelling the same Body to Motion; sometimes they conspire, sometimes are indifferent to each other, and sometimes are in some degree opposite."[6] By insisting on the equal importance of private advantage and public good, with the former not diminishing the benevolence of the action, and with the latter not being hurtful to the individual, Hutcheson opened the way for the Scottish writers who followed him to sustain a practical and utilitarian view that was neither excessively ideal nor excessively perverse.

In *Observations upon Liberal Education* George Turnbull cautions youth "against attempting to form theories, whether of moral or natural things by the force of imagination," and insists that the young ought to "be inured to study mankind in real life or history," where man can be seen in his worst colors, "savage, ferocious, or cruel," but also in his best, impelled to "compassion and benevolence." Turnbull describes two great passions within the human breast: the desire for liberty, but also the desire to dominate —the latter being "natural to mankind, and a passion that ought not to be erased but cherished," for it is "a necessary spur to industry and improvement, and the chief spring of all our motions. Ancient masters did not therefore dream of weeding it out, but carefully applied themselves to give it a right turn, and to improve it. . . ." As a consequence, Turnbull insists in his educational treatise that youth "ought to be early taught to take a just view of human nature, and to consider man as he really is, neither as a merely sensitive being, nor as a merely intellectual or moral one, but as a compound of moral and sensitive powers and affections."[7]

James Beattie also recognizes the prevalence of these two not necessarily antithetical qualities in man, observing that "the passions may be divided into *selfish* and *benevolent:* the former aim at our own good, the latter at the good of others." In an extended explication of Pope's line, Beattie observes that good for the species must be identical with good for the individual:

> A rational desire of our own happiness, which may be called *self-love,* is a powerful and useful propensity, and when rightly managed tends to happiness universal. In this respect "true self-love and social are the same." For that must be beneficial to the species, which, without injury to any, promotes the good of the individual; even as that which removes disease from one of the limbs contributes to the health of the whole body. Self-love, when excessive, or when injurious to others, may be called *selfishness,* and is a hateful disposition.[8]

Lord Kames makes this identical insistence on the reciprocity between benevolence and self-love. "According to some writers, man is entirely a selfish being: according to others, universal benevolence is his duty: one founds morality upon sympathy solely, and one upon utility," Kames writes in *Elements of Criticism.* In "confuting such Utopian systems," he observes that "benevolence may not improperly be said to be the most refined selfishness." Man's "constitution partly selfish, partly social, fits him much better for his present situation" in society, Kames explains. Since man's constitution consists of both elements, the problem is one of education, of refining the taste, so that one can distinguish what is suitable and proper. With a perspective that is primarily esthetic, Kames offers a caustic rejection of Hobbes. "Delicacy of taste tends no less to invigorate the social affections, than to moderate those that are selfish," for it is the function of taste

> to moderate the selfish affections. By sweetening and harmonizing the temper, it is a strong antidote to the turbulence of passion, and violence of pursuit. . . . Delicacy of taste necessarily heightens our feeling of pain and pleasure; and of course our sympathy, which is the capital branch of every social passion.

This same view is sustained in Lord Kames's *Sketches of the History of Man,* where he insists that Shaftesbury's "system of universal

benevolence, is no less contradictory to experience" than Helvetius'
"selfish system." Examining each of these contradictory views,
Kames decides that "man in fact is a complex being, composed of
principles, some benevolent, some selfish: and these principles are
so justly blended in his nature, as to fit him for acting a proper part
in society." Common-sense observation, it is contended, reveals
that "universal benevolence, inculcated by several writers as a moral
duty, is discovered to have no foundation in the nature of man."
Dissocial passions are everywhere in evidence; but the social passions are equally evident. "What conclusion are we to draw from
the foregoing facts, so inconsistent in appearance with each other?"
Kames asks. "I am utterly at a loss to reconcile them, otherwise than
by holding man to be a compound of principles and passions, some
social, some dissocial."[9]

In *Essays on the History of Mankind* James Dunbar, survey-
ing the rise of civil societies, marks a point where "the brutality of
the savage begins to vanish. Some refinement appears. An appetite
for society ripens, which afterward must be gratified as well as other
appetites." Yet, primitive states are not devoid of benevolent feelings, but on the contrary, "mark, in some striking examples, the in-
violable fidelity of social love." And despite all the inventions and
improvements concomitant with civilization, self-love and egotism
still persist today, so that "it may be questioned, whether the en-
largement of our faculties, and all the advantages from arts, counter-
balance the feuds and animosities which they soon introduced into
the world." By insisting that "degeneracy, as well as improvement, is
incident to man," and that "the transition from barbarism to civility
is not more incident to mankind than the contrary transition," Dunbar forms a reply to those who contended that either self-love or
benevolence, one to the exclusion of the other, was man's natural
state, and that the advent of society is to be seen as the responsible
agent for the ensuing admixture.[10]

Adam Ferguson, adopting a position almost paralleling Dunbar's, objects to the false "division of our appetites into benevolent
and selfish, [which] has probably, in some degree, helped to mislead

our apprehension on the subject of personal enjoyment and private good," and therefore distorted our view of men and of history. ". . . In reality, the gratification of every desire is a personal enjoyment, and its value being proportioned to the particular quality or force of the sentiment, it may happen that the same person may reap a greater advantage from the good fortune he has procured to another, than from that he has obtained for himself."[11]

Although Ferguson's perspective, like Dunbar's, is historical and social, it appears obvious that their position on the ethical controversy raging in the eighteenth century is almost identical with that assumed by Hutcheson and Beattie, with their philosophical interests; by Kames, with his esthetic perspective; by Turnbull, with his educational point of view; and, more pointedly, by Smollett, who, from his literary vantage point in *Sir Launcelot Greaves*, could interpret human thought and action through a necessary interweaving of social- and self-love.

2. TWO BASIC MOTIFS are perceptible in the character of Sir Launcelot Greaves from the beginning of the novel—a public interest and a private interest. The public interest, seemingly rising from an innate love of the social virtues, leads him almost from the outset to pursue the enemies of benevolence and decorum with an extravagance that increasingly threatens both his person and his position. The private interest, a love for the peerless Aurelia Darnel, which is frustrated first by her guardian's opposition and then by her own rejection, hurls him into a madness which threatens his reason. In an ostensible attempt to submerge frustrated private interests before greater public goals, Launcelot turns to knight-errantry.

Since his chivalry is formed from the extravagance of the one and the madness of the other, it leads him into yet a third failing—a lawlessness, which ironically perverts the public motif he pursues. Before the close of the novel, if the protagonist is to achieve any degree of happiness and success, he must recognize the necessity for

reconciling public with private interests. He must abandon all hope
for Aurelia Darnel, or he must gain her, and thereby rid himself of
the madness. He must learn to practice his benevolence with decorum, and thereby rid himself of the extravagance. He must abandon the role of knight-errant, and thereby rid himself of lawlessness.

Sir Launcelot's public interest is revealed most recognizably
in his practising benevolence. At seventeen, having just returned
from the University, young Launcelot proved "to every cottager in
the parish he was a bounteous benefactor." His godson, Tom
Clarke, describes him:

> He was, in the literal sense of the word, a careful overseer of the poor;
> for he went from house to house, industriously inquiring into the
> distresses of the people. He repaired their huts, clothed their backs,
> filled their bellies, and supplied them with necessaries for exercising
> their industry and different occupations.

Though his father earlier has doubts about his son's disposition, he
grows increasingly convinced of his "feeling heart" and is pleased
to see "proofs of his son's generosity." In no time, under the aegis
of young Launcelot, the parish had undergone a social reform. "The
poor's rate was reduced to a mere trifle; and one would have thought
the golden age was revived in Yorkshire" (pp. 28-31).

The reader encounters diverse attestations of the knight's generosity from the beginning. Tom Clarke calls him "the best-natured,
worthy, generous gentleman" (p. 22). The clergyman Jenkins and
his five children, whom Greaves provides with a living, find ample
cause to commend his "generosity" and "benevolence" (p. 52). The
widow Oakley, rescued from prison and reunited with her son
through the efforts of Sir Launcelot, concurs that "the family of
Greaves were always virtuous, humane, and benevolent"; and just
as his mother before had been her "benefactress," so now Sir
Launcelot is her "kind benefactor" (pp. 137-38). Aurelia Darnel,
rescued from a tyrannous guardian and a mercenary lover through
Launcelot's graces, insists that "a whole life spent in acknowledgment will scarce suffice to demonstrate a due sense of his goodness"

(p. 268). By the closing paragraphs of the novel, it is conceded that Launcelot and his new bride were both

> admired, esteemed, and applauded by every person of taste, senti-
> ment, and benevolence; at the same time beloved, revered, and almost
> adored by the common people, among whom they suffered not the
> merciless hand of indigence or misery to seize one single sacrifice.
> (p. 286)

Sir Launcelot is obviously a perfect representative of Shaftes-burian principles, which assume the naturalness of altruism and gregariousness, a "sense of right and wrong . . . being as natural to us as natural affection itself, and being a first principle in our constitution and make."[12] Unfortunately, he is so thoroughly im-bued with these principles that he carries them to excess. As a result, he becomes involved in numerous extravagances with an ensuing loss of decorum, both personal and social.

To his father, the country gentleman concerned with social hierarchy, Launcelot's excessive generosity is forgivable, but not the attendant proclivity for "keeping company with rooks and beggars." Thus, the father is "not angry at his spending his money, but at squandering away his time among the dregs of the people." The old knight's son appears "wholly attached to . . . lowly pleasures, while he industriously shunned all opportunities of appearing in that superior sphere to which he was designed by nature and by fortune" (pp. 26-31).

Young Launcelot's extravagance, however, is attended not only by a failure to take his place in his own personal "superior sphere," but simultaneously by a flouting of degree within society itself, for "his generosity seemed to overleap the bounds of discre-tion, and even in some cases might be thought tending to a breach of the king's peace." He forces the son of a rich farmer to wed a poor cottager's debauched daughter. He horsewhips husbands who have maltreated their wives. He violently avenges himself on a dis-reputable country lawyer, whose land borders his own estate, by "making waste among his hay and corn, sometimes by instituting suits against him for petty trespasses." He combines the roles of judge and prosecutor, for he "took the execution of the law in his own hand," and "acted as the general redresser of grievances" (pp. 53-58).

Whereas Sir Launcelot's extravagance derives from a moral sense which is responsible for his social virtues, his madness rises from a passionate love for Aurelia Darnel, who represents his private or personal interest. The moral sense is socially and altruistically oriented; the passionate love aims at fulfilling a self-interest which is so strong that, once it is denied, it upsets any due proportion between the passions and the understanding. Launcelot is "so much transported" at his first meeting with Aurelia Darnel that he cannot avoid "disclosing a passion." Her mother recognizes that their "passion is mutually sincere," but dies before a union can be consummated and the passions gratified. Her guardian, bitterly opposed to the marriage, carries her off to the country and manages to sever all correspondence between the lovers. "It was then we thought Mr. Launcelot a little disordered in his brain, his grief was so wild, and his passion so impetuous," Tom Clarke confides. Since "his whole soul was engrossed," he becomes "violently agitated by his passion for Aurelia." A temporary respite abroad, after he believes he has murdered Aurelia's guardian in a duel, fails to bring him relief. Reports still drift back of "his disordered mind" (pp. 42-49). Though he himself denies that he is "visited by that spirit of lunacy" displayed in Don Quixote, it is clear from his countenance, we are told, "that his reason was a little discomposed" (pp. 15-16).

In part, Sir Launcelot's proclivity to madness is innate and inherited, for his mother was "a little touched or so" (p. 25); and his great-great-uncle, "being lunatic, had cut his throat from ear to ear" (p. 58). But mainly, as Launcelot himself explains in a lengthy discourse with his squire, madness is a distemper, "a privation or disorder of reason itself" (p. 88). For him, it is the result of "despairing love, which had actually unsettled his understanding" (p. 177).

Although his understanding may be deranged, his benevolent feelings are enhanced by the lunacy. As Sir Launcelot observes, "madness and honesty are not incompatible—indeed, I feel it by experience" (p. 81). As a result, in order to enhance his social virtues, in which he has been eminently successful, and to divert his private passion, in which he has been seemingly unsuccessful, Sir Launcelot turns to chivalry. His determination is "to proceed in the career of adventure, and endeavour to forget the unkindness of his mistress amidst the avocations of knight-errantry" (p. 152).

Consequently, he has himself fitted with his family armor. His shield bears the emblazonment of "the moon in her first quarter, with the motto, *Impleat orbem.*" A knight, who himself "cannot be proved *compos mentis,*" officiates at the ceremony, which takes place during the festival of St. George. The best sorrel in the stables is led forth and denominated Bronzomarte. The worst servant in his employ, one Timothy Crabshaw—"universally hated among the servants, for his abusive tongue and perverse disposition . . . as strong as an elephant [but with] . . . no more courage naturally than a chicken"—is chosen for his squire. Thus equipped, and known as the Knight of the Crescent, Launcelot sets out on his first adventure (pp. 58-60). As the physician Fillet observes, "nothing was wanting to render him a complete knight-errant, but some celebrated beauty, the mistress of his heart . . . [for] love was the soul of chivalry" (p. 21).

Although knight-errantry serves a negative function, to submerge private passions and self-interests, it also functions positively, to promote Sir Launcelot's passion for public virtue. The young knight himself attests to his motives:

> I have begun my career, a candidate for honest fame; determined, as far as in me lies, to honour and assert the efforts of virtue; to combat vice in all her forms, redress injuries, chastise oppression, protect the helpless and forlorn, relieve the indigent, exert my best endeavours in the cause of innocence and beauty, and dedicate my talents, such as they are, to the service of my country.

Replying to the cynic Ferret, who sees in the Knight of the Crescent only an affected imitation of Don Quixote, whose madness

led to quarrels with windmills, the knight insists that his is an ethical battle: "I quarrel with none but the foes of virtue and decorum,
against whom I have declared perpetual war, and them I will everywhere attack as the natural enemies of mankind" (pp. 15-16).

One of his principal enemies, the young knight announces, is
a man whom he has never met, "an old, rancorous, incorrigible instrument of sedition," named Ferret. Luckily, Ferret has concealed
his identity from the gathering at the inn, for Laucelot vows to
crush this man "like an ungrateful viper, that gnawed the bosom
which warmed it into life!" (pp. 20-21). For all his extravagant
benevolence, Sir Launcelot fails to recognize the close parallel
between the "perpetual war" he himself has declared against enemies of virtue and decorum, and the *bellum omnium contra omnes*
declared by the avowed Hobbesian, Ferret, who says of himself:

> I look upon mankind to be in a state of nature; a truth, which Hobbes
> has stumbled upon by accident. I think every man has a right to
> avail himself of his talents, even at the expense of his fellow-crea-
> tures; just as we see the fish, and other animals of the creation, de-
> vouring one another. . . . (p. 276)

Though the sources of their principles may differ, the methods of
Ferret the Hobbesian and Launcelot the Shaftesburian are not too
remote. Both are engaged in a state of warfare. Both, recognizing the
inadequacy of social legislation, are pitted against the laws of the
land. Both adopt disguises to carry on this warfare: Launcelot as
knight, Ferret as mountebank and conjuror. Though Launcelot's
ends are social and legal reform—for he proposes "to act as a coadju-
tator to the law, and even to remedy evils which the law cannot
reach" (p. 18)—the means he adopts to compensate for the inadequacy of the laws bear no small similarity to Ferret's. Both are
extremists; and as we know from Smollett's antagonism in his letters
to extreme Shaftesburians,[13] and his position in *Ferdinand Count
Fathom* where he had insisted that self-love was "as universal, if not
as natural" as the social-love espoused by modern disciples of Plato,[14]
both extremes are unreasonable and unpalatable to the novelist.

This, then, is the picture of Sir Launcelot Greaves at the outset of the novel. He is a man of social virtues, but his benevolence is extravagant. He is a man with a private interest, a passion for Aurelia Darnel, but its denial has led to madness. Knight-errantry couples these two flaws, the extravagant benevolence and the madness. While intended to develop his social virtues and quell the passionate self-interest, the knight-errantry only induces a third flaw: a lawlessness which threatens both himself and society.

The discordant note struck by these three flaws—the extravagant benevolence, the madness, the lawnessness—resounds ultimately, as it does initially, on symbolic levels that merge with frequency and become almost indistinguishable. These flaws all follow parallel paths in Sir Launcelot's development through the second section of the novel. They all figure largely in the crucial recognition achieved in chapters XV-XIX. Their parallel diminution, as social virtues are harmonized with self-interests, contributes largely to the happiness and success the protagonist achieves by the close of the novel.

3. THE ETHICAL THEME—from which these three flaws rise in an increasingly dissonant crescendo—asserts itself almost at once in the opening section of the first movement (chs. I-VII). Four travelers are gathered at the Black Lion Inn, on the northern road from York to London. Three—Fillet, Crowe and Clarke—agree to pass the time over a bowl of rumbo. Ferret, who is somewhat less gregarious, refuses to join their company. This distinction between "the social triumvirate" and "the solitary guest" strikes the opening note of the ethical theme which is to reverberate throughout the novel. Once Sir Launcelot enters the Inn (ch. II) and declares his antagonism to "the foes of virtue and decorum," especially to one, Ferret, the theme is reinforced with clarity and precision.

With the introduction of Tom Clarke's narrative (chs. III-V), which reconstructs young Launcelot's past, a major variant of this externalized opposition between the "social" and the "solitary" is subtly sounded: namely, the conflict *internal* to the knight, his own inability to reconcile his feelings of social virtue with his self-interests. A minor variant, emanating from the sub-plot, is heard by the close (chs. VI-VII) of this movement, as Captain Crowe, a man of no small benevolence, announces his determination to follow Sir Launcelot's lead and become a knight-errant. Here too, in this minor variant, the discordant notes of Sir Launcelot's flaws are echoed and re-echoed; for, like the man he emulates, Captain Crowe is charged with "madness" and "extravagance." And it is no mere coincidence that from the beginning the good Captain bitterly inveighs against the laws of the land; for with the assistance of an attorney, his grandmother Jane and his aunt Bridget have cheated him out of an inheritance to which Crowe feels rightfully entitled.

Within the second movement (chs. VIII-XIX), the dissonant sounds of madness, extravagance, and lawlessness rise from the background with a deafening crescendo, as the major ethical theme is developed. Embarked on their second adventure, the knight and his squire find ready need for knight-errantry, as they rescue from highwaymen a young lady concealed in a coach. What begins as benevolence, however, ends in madness. Revealed to them as a "person disordered in her senses," the lady is in reality Sir Launcelot's love, Aurelia Darnel. The adventure itself, which had been preceded by a dialectical counterpoint between knight and squire on the distinctions between lunacy and cowardice, ends with the detention of the squire by nearby villagers who "justly entailed upon him the imputation of lunacy." The villagers have concluded that he has "lost his wits"; and before long, Crabshaw himself is willing to concede to his master, "I'se as mad as your worship" (pp. 91-93).

The knight next extends his benevolent offices to mediate between two extreme factions at a political rally, by arguing a doctrine of "moderation" and "reason." Here too he begins with good intentions—insistent that politics "ought to be determined by far other weapons than brute force and factious clamour." Paradoxically, he himself resorts to force, once his intentions become thwarted, when "Whigs and the Tories joined against this intruder, who, being neither, was treated like a monster, or chimera in politics." Once they begin to curse, threaten, and revile him, Launcelot abandons all deference to moderation and reason, "brandished his lance, and riding into the thickest of the concourse, laid about him with such dexterity and effect, that the multitude was immediately dispersed."

Ironically, Ferret, who is set up on the edge of town selling an elixir-of-long-life, holds forth to a vast audience with a strange alchemical discourse that appeals to their non-reason, their ignorance and superstitions. Whereas the knight's appeal to reason meets with failure, Ferret's appeal to non-reason is highly successful. "His speech . . . produced such an effect upon his hearers, that his whole cargo was immediately exhausted" (pp. 101-09).

Sir Launcelot learns nothing from the contrast. When he is arrested "as a violator of the public peace, who strolled about the country with unlawful arms," his first frenzied impulse is to break his way out of prison by force. He is deterred from this, only through the offices of the lawyer, Tom Clarke, who urges vengeance "without any breach of the peace" (pp. 114-15). Vengeance is speedily attained, for the magnitude of the knight's wrath is equal to the evils of the prison's magistrate, one Justice Gobble, a "miscreant, who seemed to have insinuated himself into the commission of the peace on purpose to harass and oppress his fellow-creatures" (p. 123). Like the highwaymen, and like the two factions at the political rally, Justice Gobble and his wife are obviously unprincipled and motivated by self-love; they are "foes of virtue and decorum," against whom Sir Launcelot has "declared perpetual war." Before the adventure is concluded, prisoners in the jail (several deprived of their reason, as well as of their liberty) have been released; and the Gobbles, at first through fear, later through remorse, become reformed characters.

Although Sir Launcelot has been persuaded to act against the Gobbles through law rather than force, the adventure leaves him impressed only with his chivalric role. To be sure, the knight concedes that "the laws of this country have exempted me from the disagreeable task" of "arming myself with the right of nature, [to] exterminate such villains from the face of the earth" (p. 132). But the madness, which prevents any kind of self-knowledge, does not allow him to see that he has already armed himself "with the right of nature," an act which in itself assumes the inadequacy of "the laws of this country." Thus, the adventure leaves him affected less by a faith in superior laws than by a faith in his own virtues. His successful attack on the Gobbles enhances his character with all, but especially with the knight himself:

> Even Sir Launcelot himself was elevated to an extraordinary degree of self-complacency on the fortunate issue of his adventure, and became more and more persuaded that a knight-errant's profession might be exercised, even in England, to the advantage of the community.

Mr. Fillet is filled with esteem and affection at the knight's virtue, person, and accomplishments, "dashed as they were with a mixture of extravagance and insanity." Captain Crowe is all the more persuaded that he himself must pursue the path of chivalry. The populace of the town testifies its approbation. Significantly, only the lawyer, Tom Clarke, appears unanimated by the success, for he had —and "not without good reason," Smollet notes—"laid it down as a maxim, that knight-errantry and madness were synonymous terms; and that madness, though exhibited in the most advantageous and agreeable light, could not change its nature, but must continue a perversion of sense to the end of the chapter" (p. 140).

The madness continues unabated. Sir Launcelot becomes so blinded with success that he cannot distinguish friend from foe. Following an argument with Captain Crowe about the merits of their respective mistresses, he challenges the benevolent captain to "engage with equal arms in mortal combat, that shall decide and determine this dispute" (p. 144). Before too many hours, he is engaged in yet another challenge, this time to two haberdashers, posing as officers, who, molesting two ladies at the inn, have become, in Launcelot's terms, "nuisances to society" (p. 148).

One of these ladies, unknown to Sir Launcelot, is Aurelia Darnel, fleeing from an enforced marriage to the mercenary Squire Sycamore, and from a charge of *non compos mentis* made by her tyrannical guardian. Only her lost pocketbook, restored through the offices of chivalry after a cross-country chase, brings the two lovers together to clear up earlier misunderstandings. Their reunion is only momentary, however. Before, the knight's monomaniacal pursuit of social virtues had prevented any kind of union, despite their paths having crossed on several occasions. Now, his monomania still acts as a preventive. Before they can concert any plan of conduct to gratify their mutual self-interest, sounds of distress coming from the adjacent highway arouse Sir Launcelot's chivalric disposition:

> The supposition of such distress operated like gunpowder on the disposition of our adventurer, who, without considering the situation of Aurelia, and indeed without seeing, or being capable to think on her or any other subject for the time being, ran directly to the stable, and, mounting the first horse which he found saddled, issued out in the twilight, having no other weapon but his sword. (pp. 168-69)

The calls of distress lead Sir Launcelot farther and farther away from Aurelia Darnel. The union that Chance had made possible, his extravagance and madness now deny. The cries prove only an artful ruse, initiated by Aurelia's guardian, to remove the knight from the scene, while the lady is spirited off to London.

Although Sir Launcelot Greaves is still too thoroughly preoccupied with his social virtues to bring to good purpose this meeting with Aurelia Darnel, he undergoes a noticeable change in the closing section of the novel (chs. XX-XXV). This change is most perceptible in his *ends*, now oriented toward self-interest as much as toward the social good. Now, he aims at a union with Aurelia Darnel and a gratification of his passion, as well as at a perpetuation of benevolence and decorum. But the change is also perceptible in the altered *means* he adopts to pursue these new ends—the use of reason, rather than madness; deferring to higher law, rather than acceding only to his own sense of virtue.

This change becomes apparent first in his tour of King's Bench Prison (ch. XX), where he believes Aurelia might have been confined under spurious charges by her guardian. Here, he encounters, "between two of the demagogues of the place," a battle strongly reminiscent of the strife encountered earlier at the political rally, when Whigs rose against Tories. As the guide explains of the prison, "this microcosm, or republic in miniature, is like the great world, split into factions." Ensuing quarrels have so endangered the safety of the prison that "some of the more sedate inhabitants having met and deliberated upon some remedy for these growing disorders, proposed that the dispute should be at once decided by single combat between the two chiefs." Such proceedings are necessary, the guide insists, for they are "convenient vents for the evaporation of those humours, which, being confined, might accumulate and break out with greater fury in conspiracy and rebellion" (pp. 222-23). Earlier, at the political rally, the knight had urged a doctrine of moderation, when violence threatened; now, he stands idly before the fracas and seemingly accepts the guide's statement on the necessity for faction.

His change is all the more perceptible within the madhouse, to which he has been mysteriously committed. Here "he heartily repented of his knight-errantry, as a frolic which might have very serious consequences, with respect to his future life and fortune." As a result, he is determined to avoid all indications of extravagance, for "after mature deliberation, he resolved to demean himself with the utmost circumspection, well knowing that every violent transport would be interpreted into an undeniable symptom of insanity" (p. 253).

Freed from the madhouse in which Aurelia Darnel also has been incarcerated, Launcelot reveals yet another indication of change. He turns to law rather than to his own chivalric force, to reason rather than madness, in promoting social virtues. Learning that he had been committed through the perfidy of Squire Sycamore, who is himself in pursuit of Aurelia, though more for her fortune than for her person, the knight institutes a plan of action against the Squire and his accomplice, Davy Dawdle:

> Sir Launcelot was not now so much of a knight-errant as to leave Aurelia to the care of Providence, and pursue the traitors to the farthest extremities of the earth. He practised a much more easy, certain, and effectual method of revenge, by instituting a process against them, which, after writs of *capias, alias et pluries,* had been repeated, subjected them both to outlawry. (pp. 273-74)

Only in this altered state can Sir Launcelot come to terms with the Hobbesian, Ferret, who reveals he is the lawful husband of Crowe's aunt Bridget. In the seditionist Ferret, ironically, lies the lawful means of proving "the docking of the entail of the estate of Hobby Hole was illegal and of none effect" (p. 278). Though the estate is now returned to its legal owner, Captain Crowe, this is accomplished only by securing Ferret from the hands of a bailiff who is about to send him to Bridewell as an imposter. In effect, a utilitarian bargain is struck for Ferret's release; the Shaftesburian knight comes to terms with the Hobbesian misanthrope, and benevolence is reconciled with the forces of self-love:

> Crowe, by the advice of Sir Launcelot and his nephew, entered into conditional articles with the cynic, to allow him the interest of fifteen hundred pounds for life, provided by this means the captain should obtain possession of the estate of Hobby Hole in Yorkshire, which had belonged to his grandfather, and of which he was heir of blood.
> (p. 278)

The "solitary" misanthrope agrees to become more "social," and is assigned an apartment in the knight's own house; while the "social" group, limiting the exercise of its benevolence, pursues its self-interests. Captain Crowe regains his inheritance and marries Mrs. Oakley, for whom he has revealed a passion. Tom Clarke marries Dolly Cowslip, Aurelia's compassionate companion throughout most of the adventures, who is discovered to be Dorothea Greaves, illegitimate daughter of Sir Launcelot's uncle. And Sir Launcelot himself is united with "the lady whom Heaven had destined for his consort."

This basic congruity of benevolence and self-love, social and private interests, is clearly discernible in *Elements of Moral Philosophy*, where David Fordyce points to "two Classes of Affection, the Private and Public, [which] are set one against the other, and designed to controul and limit each other's Influence, and thereby to produce a Just Balance in the Whole," with self-love "pointing to the Good of the Individual" and benevolence "to that of the Species." Correspondingly, man faces different kinds of duties: one which he owes to self, "founded chiefly on the defensive and private passions, which prompt him to pursue whatever tends to private good or happiness"; and also a "second class of duties [which] arises from the public or social affections." Like Smollett, Fordyce equally attacks "Hobbes, who . . . seems to have taken too narrow and partial a View of our Nature"; and the Cambridge Platonists, Clarke and Woolaston, who "call Morality a Conformity to Truth, [which] gives no Idea, no Characteristic of it, but what seems equally applicable to Vice."[15]

4. AURELIA DARNEL, whose appearances are frequent but fleeting, plays a role that is symbolic rather than dramatic in the novel's central chapters (XV-XIX). Unfortunately, this most crucial section, where Sir Launcelot is provided through her with a recognition of his flaws, is the weakest link in the development of architectonics. Serving a dual function here, Aurelia is the direct cause of the diminution of flaws in Sir Launcelot; but she is also the knight's new goal, the effect of that diminution.

The knight's recognition is *internal*, however, and comes about after a momentary appearance by the lady. Obviously cognizant of this dramatic weakness, Smollett has provided in these central chapters a second, and *externalized* conflict, on which the final section of the novel can pivot—the combat between the knight and Squire

Sycamore. Although the dramatic combat reinforces the attitudinal shift occasioned by the momentary meeting with Aurelia Darnel, it also dissipates the effects of this crucial "turning point" by spreading its attendant action over five chapters, a fifth of the novel's surface, rather than utilizing a single terse and concentrated "point." In addition, the internal and external conflicts are separated by an adventure with Farmer Prickle which is extraneous to Launcelot's crucial recognition and further deters development. Finally, though Smollett provides us with causes for the shifts taking place, their significances are presented only implicitly, through action rather than direct statement, and symbolically rather than rhetorically.

The loss of Aurelia Darnel had occasioned Sir Launcelot's madness. Now, the madness abates and reason returns, as he discovers her reciprocal passion and learns that an earlier note of rejection, delivered by a curious mishap into his hands, had been intended for Squire Sycamore. Though their reunion is interrupted by an artful ruse, which enables her guardian to separate the lovers and hurry Aurelia away to London, the knight recognizes in candidly scrutinizing his heart that "he found himself much less unhappy than he had been before his interview with Aurelia," because "instead of being as formerly tormented with the pangs of despairing love, which had actually unsettled his understanding, he was now happily convinced that he had inspired the tender breast of Aurelia with mutual affection." By the following day, we learn, the madness has further waned, for "as the torrent of his despair had disordered the current of his sober reflection, so now, as that despair subsided, his thoughts began to flow deliberately in their ancient channel" (pp. 177-82).

His meeting with Aurelia not only restores his reason, but leads him to abandon chivalry. He is ready to concede that "ever since his interview with Aurelia, his fondness for chivalry had been gradually abating." Therefore, he is determined to abandon his old methods, "resolving to lay aside his armour" and pursue new ends, "the interest of his passion." Now, though, he is "determined to wait with patience, until the law should supersede the authority of her guardian, rather than adopt any violent expedient which might hazard the interest of his passion" (p. 182).

These decisions, to abandon his chivalric role and operate only within legal bounds in the pursuit of this new goal, are reinforced by Sir Launcelot's combat with Squire Sycamore. Infected with knight-errantry, somewhat after the manner of Crowe, and posing as Knight of the Griffin, Sycamore challenges the protagonist to mortal combat which will determine their rivalry for Miss Darnel. Sir Launcelot, however, has already rejected unprincipled force as his guide; therefore, sanely reflecting "on the nature of the dispute, and the serious consequences it might produce, he resolved to decline the combat, as a trial of right and merit founded upon absurdity."

In the quiet of his room, Sir Launcelot faces an awareness heightened by his earlier meeting with Aurelia:

> chivalry was an useful institution while confined to its original purposes of protecting the innocent, assisting the friendless, and bringing the guilty to condign punishment. But he could not conceive how these laws should be answered by violating every suggestion of reason, and every precept of humanity. (p. 202)

This rejection of mortal combat in the name of Law, Reason, and Humanity is not too remote from Smollett's own position revealed in his *Travels*. There, he expatiates on "the absurd and pernicious custom of duelling . . . founded in diametrical opposition to common sense and humanity," and says of French officers that the "generous humanity which they exercise towards their enemies, even amidst the horrors of war . . . is the only circumstance of antient chivalry, which I think was worth preserving."[16]

The reversal in situation which Squire Sycamore induces for Launcelot has been made possible only by previous reversals in attitude, effected by Aurelia Darnel. Sycamore's challenge is rejected as "a step that contradicts my own reason as much as it would outrage the laws of my country."

Next, forced by Sycamore's belligerence to do battle, Sir
Launcelot exercises "the offices of humanity" against his antagonist,
displaying benevolence rather than vengeance. Third, once his
squire avails himself of the spoils of battle, Launcelot subjects him
"to the severest chastisement for his injustice and rapacity." Fourth,
the knight reaffirms his prior decision, "that, as the cause which had
engaged him in this way of life no longer existed, he was determined
to relinquish a profession which, in a peculiar manner, exposed him
to the most disagreeable incidents." Fifth, he announces his intentions of appearing henceforth "not in the character of a lunatic
knight-errant, but as a plain English gentleman, jealous of his
honour, and resolute in his purpose." Finally, and belatedly, he
becomes suitably metamorphosed, as he "exchanged his armour
for a riding-coat, hat, and boots," while "the armour, including the
accoutrements of the novice and the squire, were left in the care of
the innkeeper" (pp. 205-17).

With these crucial changes, effected attitudinally by Aurelia,
and effected situationally and dramatically by Sycamore, the third
movement opens. Accompanied by his party, the knight sets out for
London with one intent: the pursuit of Aurelia Darnel, "the interest of his passion." This is to be his overwhelming concern during
this concluding section of the novel.

5. A STRATEGIC ROLE is assumed by Aurelia Darnel, and
also, though secondarily, by Squire Sycamore, in effecting crucial
changes within the central section. This is perceptible, for all its
significance, on a level more symbolic than rhetorical. Although we
are presented rhetorically with the cause for as well as the nature
of Sir Launcelot's change, in attitude and situation, a rhetorical
statement of its significance is never made, nor is an evaluation of
its effect. True, significances can be inferred by unraveling the
tangled thread of action. The manner in which the protagonist is
allowed to achieve his goals, and the threats which potently prevent

achievement, both point to the ethical theme, the relationships between Sir Launcelot's public and private interests; his excessive pursuit of the former, resulting in the triple flaws of extravagant benevolence, madness, and lawlessness; the abandonment of these flaws,
as he determines to fulfill his private interest; and the ultimate reconciliation of these two interests culminating in happiness and
success.

Despite her minor dramatic role, Aurelia Darnel assumes a
meaningful part in this ethical drama. Her absence pointedly con-
notes extravagance, madness, and lawlessness; her presence con-
notes decorum, reason, and law. Without her, Sir Launcelot gives
vent to extravagant benevolence; with her, he can indulge in self-
interests, and private virtues can be reconciled with public. Without
her, Sir Launcelot gives way to madness, to the dictates of a mind
unguided by the heart, an understanding divested of spirit; with her,
he can follow reason, as the understanding of the head is reconciled
to the passions of the heart. Without her, he gives way to lawlessness, following only the dictates of his own conscience; with her, he
can acknowledge the superiority of social and political laws, and can
reconcile the temporal with the spiritual.

Symbolically embodied in Aurelia Darnel, Sir Launcelot's
need for love is delineated early in the novel, when the physician
Fillet observes that "love was the soul of chivalry," and that
"nothing was wanting to render him a complete knight-errant, but
some celebrated beauty, the mistress of his heart, whose idea might
animate his breast, and strengthen his arm to the utmost exertion
of valour" (p. 21). Launcelot himself confirms this, when he cautions Captain Crowe, who also is infected by the madness of knight-
errantry, that "love is an infallible pilot" (p. 142) and "the very
essence of chivalry" (p. 83); and that "next to the protection of
Heaven, it is from love that the knight derives all his prowess and
glory" (p. 142). Crowe is counselled that "towards the practice of
chivalry, there is something more required than the virtues of courage and generosity." This, ostensibly, is "love, whose empire he
should submissively acknowledge" (p. 83). Unaware that he is

offering a commentary on his own deficiency, Sir Launcelot describes the ideal knight:

> The bare name of his mistress invigorates his arm; the remembrance of her beauty infuses into his breast the most heroic sentiments of courage, while the idea of her chastity hedges him round like a charm, and renders him invulnerable to the sword of his antagonist. A knight without a mistress is a mere nonentity, or, at least, a monster in nature—a pilot without a compass, a ship without rudder, and must be driven to and fro upon the waves of discomfiture and disgrace.
>
> (pp. 142-43)

In Aurelia Darnel is embodied this "soul" or "essence," whose glory is second only "to the protection of heaven." Tom Clarke pictures her as a "model of perfection," a "supernatural being," "an angel in beauty," "a saint in goodness," and insists that "she and Sir Launcelot were formed by nature for each other" (pp. 36-37). The hostess at the White Hart Inn also calls her "a vision from heaven, a cherubim of beauty," "a heavenly creature" who is "something more than a human creature" (p. 150). Sir Launcelot too contends that "the perfections of my Aurelia are altogether supernatural," as he compares her splendor to that of "the meridian sun" (p. 143).

Sir Launcelot's pursuit of this "perfection" is almost Dantesque, while that of his rival, Squire Sycamore, is Plutonic. For Launcelot, the feelings Aurelia arouses are "of the purest passion that ever warmed the human breast," their love "a sacred idea throned within my heart . . . with such reverence of affection, as the devout anchorite more unreasonably pays to those sainted reliques that constitute the object of his adoration" (pp. 164-65). She is "the lady whom Heaven had destined for his consort," and "their Heaven-directed union" is "the consummation of all earthly felicity" (pp. 280-81). On the other hand, for Squire Sycamore, who is "enamoured of her fortune," she is symbolic only of the wealth attested by her name (obviously derived from the Latin, *aurum*, gold). Accordingly, Sycamore has arranged with her guardian to purchase his "interest and alliance with certain concessions." Despite his possession of a considerable estate to the north, Sycamore is "generally needy from extravagance." His extravagance stems from self-love alone, we learn, for "stimulated by his wants, and animated by his vanity" (pp. 153-54), it contrasts with Sir Launcelot's extravagance, which is stimulated by the rejection of his own wants and animated by his benevolence.

Appropriately dressed as Knight of the Griffin, having adopted for his escutcheon that beast who serves mythologically as guardian of treasures, Sycamore offers his challenge to Launcelot, Knight of the Crescent, for control of the lady. He insinuates "that he could eclipse his rival, even in his own lunatic sphere" (p. 197). The battle between the Knight of the Griffin and Sir Launcelot appears as a conflict between temporal and spiritual forces, between Sycamore's monetary ends and Launcelot's "heaven-directed" goals, resulting in the destruction of the "griffin" and the rescue of Aurelia, the "heavenly creature." Parallels may be drawn with the myth of Perseus, who slew Poseidon's sea-monster, thus rescuing Andromeda, whom he later obtained as a wife; with Malory's story of the Arthurian knight, whose name the protagonist bears, and who battled with Sir Modred, the treacherous knight, over possession of Guinevere; with Spenser's Red Cross Knight, who rendered himself worthy of marriage with Una by overcoming the dragon.

More significant perhaps are parallels with the legends of St. Michael and St. George, both famed as dragon-slayers and thus conquerors of the powers of darkness. These parallels are reinforced symbolically throughout the novel. The first meeting between Sycamore and Launcelot, and the ensuing challenge, occur significantly at an inn "distinguished by the sign of St. George of Cappadocia encountering the dragon, an achievement in which temporal and spiritual chivalry were happily reconciled" (p. 184). Sir Launcelot's vigil, preceding his knighthood, had taken place "on the evening of the festival of St. George." He was dubbed knight "in the name of God, St. Michael, and St. George" (pp. 58-59). Preceding the political rally, his squire had occasion to beg a boon "in the name of St. George" (p. 96); and following Ferret's alchemical discourse, Tom Clarke begged a boon "in the name of St. Michael and St. George" (p. 109).

The ensuing battle between the two knights, however, belatedly dramatizes this reconciliation of temporality and spirituality. Prior to Sycamore's challenge, his unexpected interview with Aurelia Darnel had already convinced Sir Launcelot of the mutuality of their love and induced a return to reason. Concomitant was the decision to abandon chivalry as a life inconsonant with the principles of law, reason, and humanity. Thus, the actual combat between the two knights is only minor.

The major conflict, which occurs internally rather than externally, represents a shift in ethical attitude rather than in situation. Strangely, its significance is dependent upon two symbolic strains, the alchemical and the chivalric. These are interfused and frequently indistinguishable, but at times they operate apart and on perceptible levels.

Smollett, of course, was not writing a serious alchemical novel, any more than he was writing a serious chivalric romance. Both the alchemy and the chivalry represent materials from contemporary English life which the novelist readily adapted for his own satiric ends—just as the expedition to Carthagena was used in *Roderick Random* to satirize British naval conditions; as the Grand Tour in *Peregrine Pickle* became the butt of satire; and as the waters at Bath in *Humphry Clinker* became the object of Smollett's satirical ends.

The turn to medieval materials during the 1760's is readily understandable. The cult of sublimity, initiated by Addison and reinforced by Burke, discerned in the Gothic a source of fear and terror. Old abbeys, the ruins of ancient castles and crumbling monasteries were arousing mystery and wonder for the "romantic" soul. Even medieval ballads and Northern heroic poetry were offering fruitful grounds for antiquarian research. Richard Hurd was finding a ready audience for his *Letters on Chivalry and Romance* in 1762, and Chatterton, Gray, Percy and Macpherson were all returning to the legends and romances of the Middle Ages for inspiration.

Smollett's use of alchemical materials during this "age of enlightenment," however, certainly appears as a major anomaly. The novelist himself records in his *History of England* that by the end of George II's reign (1760) "the study of alchymy no longer prevailed; but the art of chemistry was perfectly understood, and assiduously applied to the purposes of sophistication."[17] Smollett's use of *sophistication*, in a sense now obsolete, points to the sophistical and specious reasoning which chemistry inherited from alchemy. Despite the ground alchemical studies had lost during the previous century, the eighteenth century abounded with successful quacks, for medical charlatans such as the famous Chevalier Taylor and Joshua Ward could win confidence among the great, as well as among the poor and unlettered, with their elixirs and nostrums. The *Critical Review* (XI, 474-80) for June, 1760, devoting several pages to a newly published edition of the biography of the Chevalier Taylor, written by his son, points to the obvious notoriety of father and son, both alchemical quacks, remarking that "had the names of both been suppressed, it would have been impossible for any man acquainted with the characters of the drama to have mistaken the authors." In his editorial capacity for the *Critical Review* Smollett could have written the article, a task for which he was eminently suited, granted his own medical background. Even if Smollett did not write the article, as editor he must have read it. Since Taylor's biography appeared only weeks before Smollett supposedly wrote his tenth chapter of *Sir Launcelot Greaves*, obvious parallels between Ferret and Chevalier Taylor are too striking to be merely coincidental. Although in his portrayal of Ferret the seditionist, Smollett may have had in mind the political pamphleteer, Dr. John Shebbeare, there can be little question that he drew from Taylor or others like him in representing Ferret the alchemist and mountebank.[18]

Ferret, whose Hobbesian principles justify the use of any means in achieving his ends, has already recognized, unlike Sir

Launcelot, the folly of speaking the truth and appealing to reason, for this has only resulted in open conflict with the law and a charge of sedition. Accordingly, like the Hobbesian Fathom, he is prepared to assume any disguise to answer his ends. In his first appearance he has a small bundle hidden underneath his coat (p. 3), later revealed to contain "divers nostrums" (p. 71). Launcelot's squire almost immediately types him as "a showman or a conjurer" (p. 14); and before long, the entire company at the Black Lion Inn is convinced that before plunging into the political seas Ferret "had occasionally figured in the character of that facetious droll, who accompanies your itinerant physicians, under the familiar appellation of Merry-Andrew, or Jack-Pudding" (p. 40). He and Tom Clarke disguise themselves in a farcical interlude during Crowe's vigil as the spirits of Crowe's grandmother Jane and aunt Bridget—Tom, stimulated by fun; Ferret, "merely in the hope of seeing a fellow-creature miserable" (p. 71).

Ferret's most significant disguise, central to the crucial turning point, occurs in the tenth chapter, where he appears before a large crowd as alchemist and nostrum-monger. Beginning his oration with a denunciation of quackery in general, Ferret proceeds to an historical arraignment of Aristotle, that "pedantic blockhead," of "that wiseacre, Dioscorides . . . that crazy commentator, Galen . . . that mad scoundrel, Paracelsus . . . that visionary Van Helmont." He himself, to the contrary, has been "bred regularly to the profession of chemistry" and "tried all the processes of alchemy." With this preliminary, Ferret launches into an important distinction between *auri vulgi*, the false, non-spiritual, volatilized vitriol, and *auri nostrum*—his own "true, genuine, unadulterated, unchangeable, immaculate, and specific *chruseon pepuromenon ek puros*." His elixir, Ferret contends, "sold for no more than sixpence a phial, contains the essence of the alkahest, the archaeus, the catholicon, the menstruum, the sun, the moon."

> I may venture to say, that this here elixir is, in fact, the *chruseon pepuromenon ek puros*, the visible, glorious, spiritual body, from

whence all other beings derive their existence, as proceeding from
their father the sun, and their mother the moon; from the sun, as
from a living and spiritual gold, which is mere fire; consequently,
the common and universal first-created mover, from whence all
moveable things have their distinct and particular motions; and also
from the moon, as from the wife of the sun, and the common mother
of all sublunary things.

And forasmuch as man is, and must be, the comprehensive end
of all creatures, and the microcosm, he is counselled in the Revelation
to buy gold that is thoroughly fired, or rather pure fire, that he may
become rich and like the sun; as, on the contrary, he becomes poor,
when he abuses the arsenical poison; so that, his silver, by the fire,
must be calcined to a *caput mortuum,* which happens when he will
hold and retain the menstruum, out of which he partly exists, for his
own property, and doth not daily offer up the same in the fire of the
sun, that a woman may be clothed with the sun, and become a sun,
and thereby rule over the moon; that is to say, that he may get the
moon under his feet.   (pp. 107-08)

Although Ferret affects a spirit of reason, distinguished from
"quackery," he is actually using alchemical cant with its typical
assumptions of a mystic correspondence between the astrological,
the anatomical, and the chemical. He is skillfully following the
tendency common among alchemists to speak of metals by their
planetary names (lead as Saturn, tin as Jupiter, gold as the Sun,
silver as the Moon) and to attempt an interaction or impregnation
(between silver and gold, sulphur and mercury, etc.), in order to
obtain from the union a perfection of metals.[19] Similarly, Ferret
reveals a thorough knowledge of the medical theories of Paracelsus
and the neo-Platonists in general, who saw man (the microcosm)
as the epitome of the universe (the macrocosm), both having their
suns, and moons, and planets with predestined courses.

As the heavenly bodies could exert some influence on the health and
diseases of men, so the corresponding planets of the human organism
have similar influences. Thus, as the sun by its light and heat influences all living things, so the heart, the sun of the body, has its determined course and gives light and warmth to the body. To the moon

and its influences correspond the brain in man; similarly, the lungs correspond to Mercury, the liver to Jupiter, the kidneys to Venus, the gall to Mars, etc.[20]

Ferret is obviously delineating in his discourse the necessity of achieving "essence" from both sun and moon elements, from the heart as well as the head; but also the necessity for avoiding poisonous abuse through retaining the menstruum, holding on to the *materia*, out of which man only "partly exists," and therefore being unpurified by the sun, failing to obtain *spiritus*, neglecting the true *coniunctio*, and maintaining poverty of body and spirit.

Ferret's discourse is of course neither gibberish nor an event limited in meaning to that tenth chapter. Throughout the novel, Ferret plays a curious double role. As a seditionist, he is a symbol of illegality and an opponent of Sir Launcelot's chivalric ideals of virtue and decorum; yet, he is contemptuous of the knight-errantry and critical of Launcelot's extra-political office, which replaces the laws of social order with the dicta of individual conscience. As an alchemist, he is symbolic of non-reason; yet he derides Launcelot's lunacy and cautions him against his excesses.

That Sir Launcelot fails to heed Ferret's veiled message is due in part to the rapidity of adventures following the alchemical scene, for almost immediately after that scene the knight is arrested and thrust into Gobble's prison. Mainly, however, the failure is indicative of an organizational problem within the novel. If the adventure against Farmer Prickle (ch. XVII) were interchanged with the alchemical section (ch. X), then the novel would have assumed an organicism which in its present form is lacking. Following Sir Launcelot's meeting with Aurelia Darnel (when he returns to reason) and preceding his combat with Squire Sycamore (when he abandons chivalry), the alchemical chapter would have achieved an effect equal to its significance. Even in its present position, the chapter tends to throw much light upon Sir Launcelot's flaws. At the conclusion of Ferret's learned oration, Sir Launcelot recognizes within himself that the nostrum-monger "had mixed some melan-

choly truths with his scurrility." Though there is no indication of
the nature of these "truths," this becomes manifest in examining
the symbolic level on which the knight's recognition operates, as a
consequence of his reunion with Aurelia Darnel.

Sir Launcelot, known also as Knight of the Crescent (pp. 200,
206, 213, etc.), is pointedly identified with the alchemical moon-
symbol throughout the novel. His shield bears the emblazonment of
"the moon in her first quarter" (p. 60). His squire's cap is suitably
embroidered with "the figure of a crescent," and even the squire's
face is noticeably "the exact resemblance of a moon in the first quarter" (p. 12). Sycamore's intent in assuming the garb of knight—
to "eclipse his rival, even in his own lunatic sphere" (p. 197)—
appears to link all the references of lunacy, with which the novel
abounds, to the moon-symbol. On the more obvious level, Launcelot's identification with the moon-symbol is indicative of his lunacy,
a disease which was believed, even in the eighteenth century, particularly among the unlearned, to follow the course of the moon. But
seen in the light of Ferret's alchemical discourse, the Beatrician
nature of Aurelia's perfections, the etymology of her name, and
Launcelot's insistence almost immediately after Ferret's oration on
comparing his mistress with "the meridian sun" (p. 143)—then the
real nature of Sir Launcelot's recognition, and Aurelia Darnel's role
in this turning point, relative to his madness, become considerably
clarified.

Through Ferret's alchemy, we achieve an insight into one of
Sir Launcelot's flaws, his madness. Alchemically, the knight lacks
the sun-dominated heart, essential to the understanding, and therefore he is wholly moon-dominated and lunatic; by pursuing his
heart's interest and uniting with Aurelia Darnel, then head (of
which he only "partly exists") is joined with heart, the moon element achieves *coniunctio* with the sun element, temporal is reconciled with spiritual.

Through Sycamore's chivalry, we achieve an insight into the
second of Sir Launcelot's flaws, his lawlessness. Because Sir Launcelot lacks spiritual essence, the directive soul, the rudder of knight-

errantry, he acts with a lawlessness that admits little authority beyond his own conscience and his own chivalric powers. Union with Aurelia Darnel reconciles the laws of individual conscience with divine laws embodied in her heavenly perfections, and the individual is properly merged within society.

Both the alchemical and chivalric levels, however, operate only in a limited way in the development of the novel as a whole. They are not sustained throughout by plot. They offer only a limited, though important dimension to the protagonist's character and to the crucial recognition he achieves. Their real significance lies in their reinforcement of the ethical theme, the extravagant benevolence which Sir Launcelot discards, once he determines to pursue his self-interests. For the ultimate union between social- and self-love, public and private virtues, is a reconciliation that is not only social and moral, but deeply metaphysical, and highly spiritual.

REFERENCES

1. Walter Scott, *Lives of Eminent Novelists and Dramatists* (London, n.d.), pp. 451-52. George M. Kahrl, *Tobias Smollett*, Chicago, 1945), p. 59.

2. James Beattie, *Dissertations Moral and Critical* (Dublin, 1783), II, 316 ff.; *Essays* (Philadelphia, 1809), VI, 158-59.

3. Leslie Stephen, *History of English Thought* (New York, 1881), II, 16-17. See also Lois Whitney, *Primitivism and the Idea of Progress* (Baltimore, 1934), pp. 21-22; F. Homes Dudden, *Henry Fielding* (Oxford, 1952), II, 685.

4. Bernard Mandeville, *The Fable of the Bees*, ed. F. B. Kaye (Oxford, 1924), I, 324 ff., lxxii-lxxiii.

5. Margaret Fitzgerald, *First Follow Nature* (New York, 1947), p. 166. Walter Jackson Bate, *From Classic to Romantic* (Cambridge, Mass., 1946), pp. 48 ff.

6. Francis Hutcheson, *An Inquiry into the Original of Our Ideas of Beauty and Virtue* (London, 1729), p. 136.

7. George Turnbull, *Observations upon Liberal Education* (London, 1742), pp. 21-23, 392-93, 424.

8. James Beattie, *Elements of Moral Science* (Philadelphia, 1809), I, 197-200.

9. Henry Home, Lord Kames, *Elements of Criticism* (New York, 1838), pp. 15-33, 97. See also pp. 62 ff., 164, 451. *Sketches of the History of Man* (Edinburgh, 1778), II, 187, 200; IV, 27-29.

10. James Dunbar, *Essays on the History of Mankind* (London, 1781), pp. 3, 24-32, 189. See also pp. 32 ff., 353 ff.

11. Adam Ferguson, *An Essay on the History of Civil Society* (London, 1773), pp. 87-88.

12. Anthony Ashley Cooper, Third Earl of Shaftesbury, *Characteristics,* ed. John M. Robertson (London, 1900), I, 260.

13. Tobias Smollett, *Letters,* ed. Edward S. Noyes (Cambridge, 1926), p. 60.

14. Tobias Smollett, *Ferdinand Count Fathom,* ed. George Saintsbury (London, n.d.), II, 116-17.

15. David Fordyce, *Elements of Moral Philosophy,* in Robert Dodsley's *The Precepter* (London, 1775), II, 247, 263-69, 278-85.

16. Tobias Smollett, *Travels through France and Italy,* ed. Thomas Seccombe (London, 1919), p. 134.

17. Tobias Smollett, *The History of England* (London, 1841), IV, 458.

18. In "Smollett's Pamphleteering Foe Shebbeare," *PMLA* (1942), LVII, 1053-1100, James R. Foster argues convincingly that the portrait of Ferret is based upon Smollett's personal antagonism with Shebbeare.

19. See Herbert Silberer, *Problems of Mysticism and its Symbolism* (New York, 1917), pp. 118-21. Also Herman Boerhaave, *A New Method of Chemistry,* trans. by Peter Shaw (London, 1741). Even Boerhaave in this standard eighteenth-century text admits indebtedness for his methodology to *"Paracelsus* and *Helmont,* who are the heads of all the chemical physicians" (I, 45).

20. John Maxon Stillman, *Paracelsus* (Chicago, 1930), pp. 53 ff.

CHAPTER SIX. *HUMPHRY CLINKER*:

A Study in Primitivism and Progress

1. DURING the first half of the eighteenth century, the popularity of foreign travel, especially of the Grand Tour of France and Italy, resulted in a plethora of guidebooks, itineraries, compendiums of voyages, and books of travels. Typically, many were in the epistolary form. Henry Davis, the fictitious London bookseller whose letter affords a preface to *The Expedition of Humphry Clinker*, comments despairingly on the trend:

> There have been so many letters upon travels lately published—What between Smollett's, Sharp's, Derrick's, Thickness's, Baltimore's, and Baretti's, together with Shandy's Sentimental Travels, the public seems to be cloyed with that kind of entertainment.

With his own seven volumes of *A Compendium of Authentic and Entertaining Voyages* (1756), two volumes of *Travels through France and Italy* (1766), and eight volumes of *Present State of All Nations* (1768-69), Smollett himself was acceding to popular fashion.

When he began his seven-month tour of England and Scotland in 1766, which later was to furnish the seed for *Humphry Clinker*, Smollett was acting as forerunner of a new fad. Except for Martin Martin, John Macky, Daniel Defoe, and Edward Burt, the English writer was little concerned with domestic travel before 1760. The tide began to turn in the sixties, but as late as 1773—two years after the publication of Smollett's final novel—Samuel Johnson was commenting apologetically in *A Journey to the Western Islands of Scotland:*

> To write of the cities of our own island with the solemnity of geographical description, as if we had been cast upon a newly discovered coast, has the appearance of very frivolous ostentation; yet . . . Scotland is little known to the greater part of those who may read these observations.[1]

With similar dismay, Boswell was writing of the "simplicity and wildness, and all the circumstances of remote time or place, so near to our native great island."[2] In the same vein one of the characters in *Humphry Clinker* remarks: "What between want of curiosity and traditional sarcasms, the effect of ancient animosity, the people at the other end of the island know as little of Scotland as of Japan" (II, 47).

Though Smollett's contemporaries regarded travel materials as an essential ingredient of *Humphry Clinker*,[3] this has not deluded many. Horace Walpole denounced this work as "a party novel written by that profligate hireling Smollett to vindicate the Scots."[4] More recently, Louis L. Martz has argued that, due to a bitter resentment on the part of the novelist toward England as a result of Bute's harsh administration of the North country, the book is in part "motivated by Smollett's desire to denounce England and praise Scotland." This attitude is seemingly detected by a comparison of Smollett's earlier and impartial approach to England in *Present State* with the well-known opening paragraph in the *Travels* and with the viciously antagonistic *Adventures of an Atom*.[5] Unfortunately, conjectures about Smollett's shift in attitude after 1763 rest on the assumption that the English and Scottish sections in *Present State* must have been written by Smollett prior to that date. The novelist had contracted for the text well before 1763, but the completed edition did not reach the public until 1768-69, and there is little evidence of either date or authorship for the individual volumes. Actually, the text of *Present State* has always been attributed to the large staff of writers which Smollett is known to have directed during these years. In addition, opening remarks in the *Travels* can scarcely be taken as evidence of Smollett's change in attitude toward England. It is usually conceded that the form of the *Travels* is artificial; besides, even if we consider the opening paragraphs representative of Smollett's new attitude, then how can we account for the eulogy of England in the final letter:

> I am attached to my country, because it is the land of liberty, cleanliness, and convenience: but I love it still more tenderly, as the scene of all my interesting connexions; as the habitation of my friends, for whose conversation, correspondence, and esteem, I wish alone to live.

As for the *Adventures of an Atom,* there is no external evidence by which the anonymous work can be attributed to Smollett. Only a vague similarity in materials and methods can even suggest the likelihood of Smollett as author.[6]

The tendency to postulate a theory of the novel based on the author's intent, his biography, or parallels with previous works is made all the more questionable here by the absence of any direct statement of intention, by the paucity of biographical materials, and by the highly questionable authorship of both the *Atom* and *Present State.* Like the travel materials, political implications in *Humphry Clinker* must assume significance relative to the organizing principle of the novel itself. A number of factors, all internal to the text, must be considered in assessing the work. Even though the sympathetic treatment of Scotland and castigation of England enforce a duality of tone, this duality is not absolute, for there is clearly a partial vindication of England and a partial censure of Scotland. We must also recognize that the epistolary form provides the novel with a multiplicity of views. Alternating with Bramble's diatribes against England are Lydia's ecstasies and Jery's amusement. Bramble may bear some resemblance to the novelist, but basically he is no less fictitious than Lydia. The five letter-writers, distinct from one another in character, are bound together by their Welsh origin which distinguishes them from the English and Scots they encounter. Finally, since the novel provides some kind of progression, with attitudinal changes paralleling to some degree topographical changes, statements about England and Scotland must be considered relative to structural and thematic development. Any consideration of Smollett's attitude toward England and Scotland must necessarily take into account this relativity of views within the organic whole.

A passage crucial to this relativity of views is found in Jeremy's letter of April 18 from Hot Well, where he has encountered the famous Dr. L—n, who discourses at length, despite the general abhorrence of the company around him, about the relativity of smells:

> He observed that stink, or stench, meant no more than a strong impression on the olfactory nerves, and might be applied to substances of the most opposite qualities; that . . . the French were pleased with the putrid effluvia of animal food, and so were the Hottentots in Africa, and the savages in Greenland; and that the negroes on the coast of Senegal would not touch fish till it was rotten; strong presumptions in favour of what is generally called *stink*, as those nations are in a state of nature, undebauched by luxury, unseduced by whim and caprice; that he had reason to believe the stercoraceous flavour, condemned by prejudice as a stink, was, in fact, most agreeable to the organs of smelling. . . . He said, the inhabitants of Madrid and Edinburgh found particular satisfaction in breathing their own atmosphere, which was always impregnated with stercoraceous effluvia.
>
> (I, 20-21)

Although the learned doctor is generally derided, the sensitive Matthew Bramble himself acknowledges the validity of these observations three months later in Edinburgh:

> You are no stranger to their method of discharging all their impurities from their windows, at a certain hour of the night, as the custom is in Spain, Portugal, and some parts of France and Italy; a practice

to which I can by no means be reconciled. . . . The inhabitants
seem insensible to these impressions, and are apt to imagine the disgust that we avow is little better than affectation; but they ought to
have some compassion for strangers, who have not been used to this
kind of sufferance. . . .   (II, 53)

The distinction which the doctor draws between the inhabitants of Edinburgh, Africa and Greenland, who are more in "a state
of nature, undebauched by luxury," and the company at Hot Well,
which has been seduced "by luxury . . . whim and caprice," is
familiar to most students of the eighteenth century. It is the opposition between primitivism and the idea of progress, common to the
century, and central to any understanding of the antithesis posed
between England and Scotland in *Humphry Clinker*.

Terms of this opposition are obvious in *An Estimate of the
Manners and Principles of the Times* (1757), where John Brown
delineates the moral corruption that necessarily follows in the advanced stage of commerce, which "brings in superfluity and vast
wealth, begets avarice, gross luxury, or effeminate refinement
among the higher ranks, together with general loss of principle."
The conflict is perceptible in Boswell's *Life of Samuel Johnson*,
where Goldsmith expatiates on "the common topick, that the race
of our people was degenerated, and that this was owing to luxury";
and Johnson replies, "Luxury, so far as it reaches the poor, will do
good to the race of people; it will strengthen and multiply them.
Sir, no nation was ever hurt by luxury." Similarly, the antagonism
is central to Pope's "Epistle III to Lord Bathurst":

> Much injur'd Blunt! why bears he Britain's hate?
> A wizard told him in these words our fate:
> "At length Corruption, like a gen'ral flood,
> "(So long by watchful Ministers withstood)
> "Shall deluge all; and Av'rice, creeping on,
> "Spread like a low-born mist, and blot the Sun."

Allusions to this eighteenth-century antagonism are so multiple that it has become almost a truism that primitivism and the idea

of progress were opposing ideologies for the age. A recent and typical examination of popular as well as philosophical texts summarizes the conflict between "these two antagonistic systems of thought" between 1750 and 1815:

> The primitivistic ideology bade men look for their model of excellence to the first stages of society before men had been corrupted by civilization; the idea of progress represented a point of view that looked forward to a possible perfection in the future. The primitivistic teaching, again, extolled simplicity; the faith in progress found its ideal in an increasing complexity. The former system of thought, finally, taught an ethics based on the natural affections; the latter system was built on an intellectualistic foundation.

A natural corollary of primitivism, and an inherent part of that ideology since the earliest fables, was of course the theory of progressive degeneration. Because of the growing prosperity of England during the century, its expanding commerce and industry, wealth and its counterpart, luxury, were national problems. True, the assertion that luxury and degeneration were inseparable was not a new one, for it had permeated travel literature from the early sixteenth century. But by the eighteenth century, growing social and economic dissatisfactions renewed the discussions of luxury and coupled them with the prevalent notions about the "noble savage." They brought about "a re-evaluation of cultural refinement . . . a renewed burst of enthusiasm for simplicity, the simplicity of life according to nature."[7]

F. B. Kaye, in his introduction to Bernard Mandeville, points to the centrality of this opposition for *The Fable of the Bees:*

> The age was partly aware of this dualism, for it made an effort to reconcile its opinions by arguing that wealth could be attained without producing luxury and without depending on it. . . . But, none the less, it was obvious that in practice wealth and luxury were companions; and the contradiction between the actual pursuit of this wealth and the current moral condemnation of the luxury it involved remain.

Other writers have developed at length ramifications of this "contradiction," discernible in philosophic thought, in theology, and in English poetry of the period.[8] Travels were obviously not only a source of entertainment for the eighteenth century, but also a source of learning. They brought a knowledge of men and manners—the ancient Greek and Roman, the American Indian, the Hottentot. For some, they reinforced the belief that man's earliest and simplest condition was the best; for others, they confirmed with optimism the perfection toward which the more advanced stages of society were moving. By juxtaposing the more primitive and rural Scotland with the complex refinements of urbanized England, Smollett entered the lists of an important controversy of the age.

The position Smollett assumes in *Humphry Clinker*, however, is more closely aligned to the reconciling perspective of Adam Ferguson and the common-sense writers of the Scottish School. Avoiding the extreme views of the controversialists, Ferguson suggests in *An Essay on the History of Civil Society* that whereas luxury and corruption are invariably identified, the term *corruption,* which implies weakness of character, need not necessarily accompany an accumulation of wealth, which is what we understand by *luxury.* "Vices of men are not proportioned to their fortunes," it is explained. "Men grow equally familiar with different conditions, receive equal pleasure, and are equally allured to sensuality, in the palace, and in the cave." To contrast primitive nations with the more advanced stages of society is to pose a false opposition, for virtues and vices lie equally in both:

> We need not have recourse to a parallel between the manners of entire nations, in the extremes of civilization and rudeness, in order to be satisfied, that . . . the habits of avarice, or of sensuality, are not founded on any certain measures of wealth, or determinate kind of enjoyment. . . . The same passions for interest, or pleasure, prevail in every condition. They arise from temperament, or an acquired admiration of property; not from any particular manner of life in which the parties are engaged, nor from any particular species of property, which may have occupied their cares and their wishes.

The term *luxury* is itself highly relative. The Spartans prohibited the practice of the arts, which they assumed would lead to luxury and corruption, and therefore "the house-builder and the carpenter at Sparta were limited to the use of the axe and the saw"; yet, "a Spartan cottage might have passed for a palace in Thrace." Men see *luxury* in terms of their own age. In one condition the casuist condemns the use of a coach, in another the wearing of shoes. European clergy have denounced every innovation in dress. The styles and manners of the young are always censured by the old, while the young always ridicule the previous age. As a result, Ferguson insists:

> Luxury . . . considered as a predilection in favour of the objects of vanity, and the costly materials of pleasure, is ruinous to the human character; considered as the mere use of accommodations and conveniences which the age has procured, rather depends on the progress which the mechanical arts have made, and on the degree in which the fortunes of men are unequally parcelled, than on the dispositions of particular men either to vice or to virtue.[9]

William Robertson assumes a similar mediating view in his *History of North America*. Recognizing the opposing views about "the noble savage" expressed by Buffon and Rousseau, Robertson detects that with some natural historians and philosophers

> man never attained in America the perfection which belongs to his nature, but remained an animal of an inferior order, defective in the vigour of his bodily frame, and destitute of sensibility, as well as of force, in the operations of his mind. In opposition to . . . these, other philosophers have supposed that man arrives at his highest dignity and excellence long before he reaches a state of refinement; and, in the rude simplicity of savage life, displays an elevation of sentiment, an independence of mind, and a warmth of attachment, for which it is vain to search among the members of polished societies. They seem to consider that as the most perfect state of man which is the least civilized. . . . These contradictory theories have been proposed with equal confidence, and uncommon powers of

genius and eloquence have been exerted, in order to clothe them
with an appearance of truth.

Accordingly, in Book IV of his *History* Robertson projects a more
realistic picture of the American savage, aimed at dispelling these
"contradictory theories." "In the simplicity of the savage state . . .
man is not oppressed with labour, or enervated by luxury, or dis-
quieted with care," Robertson writes; he is "exempt from many of
the distempers which afflict polished nations. None of the maladies,
which are the immediate offspring of luxury, ever visited them.
. . ." But, since man is born to suffer, regardless of the situation in
which he is placed, his diseases in this savage state, though fewer
in number, are more violent and more fatal. "If luxury engenders
and nourishes distempers of one species, the rigour and distresses
of savage life bring on those of another." When he considers the
general character of American savages, Robertson readily appre-
hends that their intellectual powers are limited, their familial affections minimal, and they are frequently taciturn, melancholy, and
given to cunning. "But if there be defects or vices peculiar to the
savage state, there are likewise virtues which it inspires, and good
qualities, to the exercise of which it is friendly," Robertson adds.
Thus, the primitive state is conducive to a greater spirit of inde-
pendence than is generally found among polished nations; there is
greater fortitude and valor, a passionate attachment to the community, and a larger satisfaction with one's own condition than is
found among most Europeans. As a result, Robertson's savage is
neither completely noble nor completely ignoble, but comprehends
both vices and virtues.[10]

Lord Kames offers almost the same kind of cultural relativity
in *Sketches of the History of Man*, where he observes that "every
historian, ancient and modern, while he inveighs against the luxury
of his own times, wonders at former historians for characterizing as
luxury what he considers as conveniences merely, or rational improvements." This, Kames attributes to a confusion in terminology.

With a wealth of examples he reveals that "every improvement in living is pronounced to be luxury while recent, and drops that character when it comes into common use. For the same reason, what is moderation in the capital, is esteemed luxury in a country-town." The term *luxury*, Kames suggests, is properly derived from the "general proposition, That every indulgence in corporeal pleasure, which favours either too violent or too languid exercise, whether of mind or body, is hurtful." Such indulgence is judged by the moral sense:

> In the hot climates of Asia, people of rank are rubbed and chaffed twice a-day; which, beside being pleasant, is necessary for health, by moving the blood in a hot country, where sloth and indolence prevail. The Greeks and Romans were curried, bathed, and oiled, daily; tho' they had not the same excuse for that practice: it was luxury in them, tho' not in the Asiatics.

Generally, luxury is indiscriminately condemned from our own ignorance about its real ethical nature, Kames explains; for the same reason, peace is indiscriminately lauded. Yet, wealth, like industry, is but an offspring of peace, and frequently in an advanced society "man by constant prosperity and peace degenerates into a mean, impotent, and selfish animal. An American savage . . . is a being far superior. Such are the fruits of perpetual peace with respect to individuals." Despite artistic and scientific progress, civilized man is capable of degenerating, just as primitive man is capable of ascending to noble and admirable heights. This is apparent, Kames says, with the North American savages among whom "mutual affection prevails, because there is no cause of discord"; and with the rude inhabitants of the Philippines who "are better fitted for society than any other known nation. Sweetness of temper, and love to do good, form their character."[11]

Reconciliations offered here by Ferguson, Robertson and Kames are strikingly similar, not only to one another, but to those offered by Hugh Blair, Lord Monboddo, James Dunbar, John Ogilvie—and, significantly, by Smollett. Disdaining either extreme, and suggesting a compatibility of poverty and wealth, simplicity and complexity, Smollett offers in *Humphry Clinker* a perspective most closely aligned with these writers in the last half of the eighteenth century who were centered around Edinburgh, that "hot-bed of genius" to which Matt Bramble alludes.

2. OF THE EIGHTY-TWO LETTERS that comprise *Humphry Clinker*, over two-thirds are written by Matthew Bramble, the cantankerous old squire from Wales who heads the expedition, and his young nephew, Jeremy Melford, who is fresh from the university at Oxford. Eleven are written by Jery's sister, the romantic Lydia; while six are penned by Bramble's spinster sister, Tabitha, and ten by Winifred Jenkins, her maid. Despite this disproportion, all five letter-writers serve equally as protagonists. We are concerned no less with the adventures and changes of Tabitha than we are with those of her brother. Smollett avoids undue emphasis upon any one of these major figures by titling the novel after a minor character. He focuses instead upon one of the central causes for their change, as symbolized in the simple and almost primitive Humphry Clinker.

Stated most boldly, the "expedition" is of two kinds—the superficial and the symbolic. Superficially, the expedition is a geographic journey; as such, it is the expedition of Matt Bramble, Tabitha, Jery, Lydia, and Winifred, alike. But symbolically, the expedition is a moral journey which culminates in the *expediting* or *freeing* of Humphry Clinker from the fetters of poverty, hunger, nakedness, and anonymity. The relationship between these two levels of discourse should become increasingly clear during the course of analysis.

Perhaps a major unifying device for all the central characters is their common Welsh origin. Matthew Bramble contrasts the *"compound of villanous smells"* at Bath with "the pure, elastic, animating air of the Welsh mountains. *O Rus, quando te aspiciam"* (I, 85). From London he comments at length on "the difference between my town grievances and my country comforts": the "clear, elastic, salutary air" in Wales and the "frowsy lodgings, where . . . I breathe the steams of endless putrefaction" in London; the "cordial effusions of unreserved friendship" in Wales and "the society of London . . . too much engrossed by schemes of interest or ambition, to have any room left for sentiment or friendship" (I, 153-61). In Scotland he feels a certain kinship, because he discerns "particulars, that smack of our Welsh language and customs"; and he writes from Cameron that "this country would be a perfect paradise, if it was not, like Wales, cursed with a weeping climate, owing to the same causes in both, the neighbourhood of high mountains, and a westerly situation" (II, 92-96). When Lydia complains of a headache at Bath, her aunt attributes it to "the effect of a vulgar constitution, reared among woods and mountains" (I, 53); and when a physician prescribes Highland air and goat-milk whey for Lydia's illness in Edinburgh, Bramble comments that this "surely cannot have a bad effect upon a patient who was born and bred among the mountains of Wales" (II, 76). Lydia herself writes from London that she longs again "for country solitude, and a happy retreat with those we love" (I, 123). Even the sophisticated Jeremy feels nostalgia, as he writes from Argyleshire: "The peasants of these hills strongly resemble those of Wales in their looks, their manners, and habitations; everything I see, and hear, and feel, seems Welsh—the mountains, vales, and streams; the air and climate; the beer, mutton, and game are all Welsh" (II, 83).

Although the reader is provided with knowledge of the simplicity of Welsh rural life as a gauge for evaluating the letters, this unified view is somewhat mitigated by basic differences in character.

Lydia, who joins the expedition from her boarding school at Gloucester, is young, inexperienced and romantic. Her brother finds her "a fine tall girl of seventeen, with an agreeable person; but remarkably simple, and quite ignorant of the world" (I, 8). This is confirmed by Win Jenkins, who says Lydia is "as innocent as the child unborn" (I, 54), and by her uncle and guardian, Matt Bramble, who describes her as "a simple girl utterly unacquainted with the characters of mankind" (I, 16). Bramble perceives that she "reads romances," and though she is no fool, "she is a poor good-natured simpleton, as soft as butter, and as easily melted" (I, 13). Having been restrained for months in her boarding school, she has already been "melted" by an actor, Wilson. The frantic attempts of the lovers to communicate, despite objections from Lydia's family, especially her brother Jeremy, form the first of a series of subplots running throughout the novel. Once it is discovered that "Wilson" is really George Dennison, son of a country squire who is Bramble's friend, the adventure culminates in marriage.

At Hot Well, Lydia finds the pastoral Downs "a charming romantic place"; but most of the time "for variety" she goes down to Bristol spring, which "afford[s] such an enchanting variety of moving pictures" (I, 33). For Lydia, Bath is "a new world. All is gaiety, good-humour, and diversion." Here, "the eye is continually entertained with the splendour of dress and equipage, and the ear with the sound of coaches, chaises, chairs, and other carriages" (I, 49). In London, too, her "imagination is quite confounded with splendour and variety." With a vocabulary typical of the new cant of sublimity, Lydia finds St. Paul's "grand and magnificent," the prospect "grand and astonishing," the "three stupendous bridges . . . so vast, so stately, so elegant," the wharves "a prodigious forest of masts." Here is "all that you read of wealth and grandeur, in the Arabian Nights Entertainment, and the Persian Tales," she writes to her dear Letty. Ranelagh seems "like the enchanted palace of a genie." Vauxhall leaves her "dazzled and confounded with the variety of beauties that rushed all at once upon my eye . . . exhibiting a wonderful assemblage of the most picturesque and striking objects, pavilions, lodges, groves, grottoes, lawns, temples, and cascades; porticoes, colonnades, and rotundas." Although she knows her uncle disapproves of London, Lydia realizes that "people of experience and infirmity . . . see with very different eyes than those that such as you and I make use of" (I, 119-21).

Her brother, recently out of the university at Oxford, is described by his uncle as "a pert jackanapes, full of college petulance and self-conceit; proud as a German count, and as hot and hasty as a Welsh mountaineer" (I, 13). Lydia has ample evidence of Jeremy's "passionate temper" (I, 12), since he impetuously stifles all correspondence with Wilson. Bramble calls him a "rash boy" (I, 14) and knows that this "hotheaded boy is more than ever incensed against Wilson, whom he . . . considers as an imposter that harbours some infamous design upon the honour of his family" (I, 189). Sufficiently astute to recognize that "the fumes of faction not only disturb the faculty of reason, but also pervert the organs of sense" (I, 124), Jeremy does not learn how much his judgment has been colored by his passions until the close of the novel. His eventual reconciliation with Wilson and the abandonment of prejudice and passion form the second sub-plot.

Unlike Lydia, whose romantic disposition thrills to the strangeness and variety of the scenes before her, Jeremy finds his delight in diversions afforded by the manners of the company surrounding him. At Hot Well he is "much diverted" with the conversations in the pump-room (I, 20). At Bath, where Bramble's "singularities afford a rich mine of entertainment," he admits being "diverted by his little distresses" (I, 35). To an extent, Jeremy is motivated by a desire to entertain his correspondent, Sir Watkin Phillips, but primarily he searches for his own amusement. He finds Bath not "without variation" and is "amazed to find so small a place so crowded with entertainment and variety." The multiplicity that Lydia finds enchanting, and that Bramble finds chaotic, is "a source of infinite amusement" for Jeremy. He is pleased by everything, as long as it serves "to heighten the humour in the farce of life, which I am determined to enjoy as long as I can." The follies which Lydia cannot discern, and which move Bramble's spleen, admittedly "excite my laughter" (I, 62-63). At Bath he revels in "the temple of mirth and good fellowship," engrossed by the wit of Mr. James Quin, the "extravagantly entertaining" actor (I, 76-77). In London he finds an assembly of Grub Street writers "very diverting" (I, 162). He discovers that "Harrowgate treads upon the heels of Bath, in the articles of gaiety and dissipation—with this difference, however, that here we are more sociable and familiar" (I, 210); as a result, he finds "the manner of living at Harrowgate . . . agreeable to my disposition," and leaves the place with much regret (I, 226). At Scarborough, happily, "diversions are pretty much on the same footing . . . as at Bath" (I, 233).

Tabitha Bramble is a spinster of forty-five, "exceedingly starched, vain, and ridiculous" (I, 9), according to Jeremy, who writes that she is "of all antiquated maidens the most diabolically capricious [and is] ever prying into other people's affairs" (I, 27). He offers a lengthy portrait of Tabby, not without some degree of objectivity:

> In her temper, she is proud, stiff, vain, imperious, prying, malicious, greedy, and uncharitable. In all likelihood her natural austerity has been soured by disappointment in love, for her long celibacy is by no means owing to her dislike of matrimony; on the contrary, she has left no stone unturned to avoid the reproachful epithet of old maid. . . . Her avarice seems to grow every day more and more rapacious. But even this is not so intolerable as the perverseness of her nature, which keeps the whole family in disquiet and uproar. She is one of those geniuses who find some diabolical enjoyment in being dreaded and detested by their fellow-creatures. (I, 78-79)

Though Matthew Bramble calls her "the devil incarnate, come to torment me for my sins" (I, 13), he also admits that his sister Tabby "is become insensibly a part of my constitution—D—n her, she's a *noli me tangere* in my flesh, which I cannot bear to be touched or tampered with." Despite her defects, Tabitha has a real attachment to her brother, "though her love never shows itself but in the shape of discontent; and she persists in tormenting him out of sheer tenderness" (I, 79-80).

Because of her avarice, Tabby's letters are never concerned with either the places that transport Lydia or the people who amuse Jeremy. They are totally preoccupied with domestic problems in Wales, expressive of her fears about extravagance and waste at home. Primarily through the letters of others, we know that Tabby looks upon England and Scotland only as matrimonial hunting-grounds. Her ardent search for a mate provides the novel with a third sub-plot. She aims her charms at Sir Ulic Mackilligut in Bath, at Mr. Barton in London, at Mr. Micklewhimmen in Harrowgate; and she turns her attention with ultimate success, in Newcastle-upon-Tyne and in Morpeth, to Obadiah Lismahago, who has just returned from the Indian wars in America.

Winifred Jenkins, Tabby's Welsh maid, serves frequently as a confidant to Lydia, who knows her as "a good girl" (I, 11), but also as a "poor creature . . . weak in her nerves, as well as in her understanding" (II, 108). Jeremy observes that Win is "tender-hearted and benevolent, qualities for which her mistress is by no means remarkable." Younger and more personable than Tabitha, Win bears a marked resemblance to her mistress, one which custom and habit have effected:

> She seems to have adopted Mrs. Tabby's manner with her cast clothes. She dresses and endeavours to look like her mistress, although her own looks are much more engaging. She enters into her schemes of economy, learns her phrases, repeats her remarks, imitates her style in scolding the inferior servants, and, finally, subscribes implicitly to her system of devotion.   (II, 40)

Understandably, Winifred is an odd compound of virtue and vanity. The former attracts her to the simplicity and integrity of Humphry Clinker; the latter is in turn appealing to Clinker's reforming spirit. Her relationship with him culminates in marriage and provides the novel with a fourth sub-plot.

Because of her simplicity, Winifred Jenkins is half-frightened and half-overawed at the scenes which transport Lydia. Like her mistress, Win writes with an abundance of malapropisms. She is impressed by "all the fine shows of Bath; the Prades, the Squires, and the Circlis, the Crashit, the Hottogon, and Bloody Buildings, and Harry King's Row"; but at the same time she is appalled at the thought of having been "twice in the bath with mistress, and na'r a smoak upon our backs, hussy." She writes to Mary Jones at Bram-

bleton that "you that live in the country have no deception of our
doings at Bath. Here is such dressing, and fiddling, and dancing,
and gadding, and courting, and plotting—O gracious!" (I, 54). In
London, too, her simplicity is overpowered by the immensity of
it all:

> O Molly, what shall I say of London? All the towns that ever I
> beheld in my born days are no more than Welsh barrows and crum-
> lecks to this wonderful sitty! Even Bath itself is but a fillitch, in the
> naam of God, one would think there's no end of the streets, but the
> Lands End. Then there's such a power of people, going hurry skurry!
> Such a racket of coxes! Such a noise and hali-balloo! So many strange
> sites to be seen! O gracious! my poor Welsh brain has been spinning
> like a top ever since I came hither!   (I, 141)

Matthew Bramble, the elderly squire who heads the expedition, is by far its most complex member. At first, Bramble is "always
on the fret, and . . . unpleasant in his manner" (I, 9), but Jeremy
soon learns that "his peevishness arises partly from bodily pain, and
partly from a natural excess of mental sensibility" (I, 20). Bramble
himself recognizes that "my spirits and my health affect each other
reciprocally—that is to say, everything that discomposes my mind,
produces a correspondent disorder in my body" (I, 202). Bramble's
search for mental and bodily health provides the novel with a fifth
sub-plot. Confronted with multiplicity and disorder in his own
household, as well as in the places he visits in England, Bramble
presents a strange mixture of benevolence and misanthropy, good
humor and the ventings of his spleen.

Jeremy offers an accurate picture of his uncle:

> His understanding, so far as I can judge, is well cultivated; his ob-
> servations on life are equally just, pertinent, and uncommon. He
> affects misanthropy, in order to conceal the sensibility of a heart
> which is tender even to a degree of weakness. This delicacy of feeling,
> or soreness of the mind, makes him timorous and fearful, but then
> he is afraid of nothing so much as of dishonour; and although he is
> exceedingly cautious of giving offence, he will fire at the least hint
> of insolence or ill-breeding. . . . Our aunt Tabitha acts upon him

as a perpetual grindstone; she is, in all respects, a striking contrast
to her brother. . . . (I, 35)

Lydia, too, for all her lack of understanding, feels "a thousand pities
he should ever be troubled with . . . distemper," for she knows
that "when he is free from pain, he is the best tempered man upon
earth; so gentle, so generous, so charitable, that everybody loves
him" (I, 51). On the other hand, Tabitha is inclined to think him
a little mad:

> My brother is little better than noncompush. He would give away the
> shirt off his back, and the teeth out of his head; nay, as for that
> matter, he would have ruinated the family with his ridiculous chari-
> ties, if it had not been for my four quarters.—What between his
> wilfulness and his waste, his trumps, and his frenzy, I lead the life
> of an indented slave. (I, 56)

Yet, we know enough of Tabitha's avarice to doubt the validity of
her judgment, just as we know we can trust Jeremy's perceptions
when they are not activated by his passions, and as we know we can
trust Lydia's feelings when they are not carried away by her
imagination.

Because of his physical and mental abhorrence of multiplicity
and disorder, Bramble reveals in his letters a consistent uniformitarianism and love of order. The variety in England that Tabitha
ignores, that awes Winifred, that Lydia finds a source of sublimity,
and that Jeremy seeks as a constant diversion and amusement, is for
Bramble a perpetual irritant and the cause of pain and unhappiness.
He is irritated at the buildings in Bath, "contrived without judgment, executed without solidity, and stuck together with . . . little
regard to plan and propriety." Disorder is social, as well as archi-
tectural, for at Bath "a very inconsiderable proportion of genteel
people are lost in a mob of impudent plebeians, who have neither
understanding nor judgment, nor the least idea of propriety and
decorum" (I, 45-47). In the public rooms is assembled a "general
mixture of all degrees . . . without distinction of rank or fortune."
This is an assembly condemned by Bramble "as a monstrous jumble

of heterogeneous principles; a vile mob of noise and impertinence, without decency and subordination" (I, 62). It is a "mixture of people . . . destructive of all order and urbanity," for it renders the plebeian arrogant and vulgarizes the sentiments of the upper classes. In London Bramble complains "there is no distinction or subordination left. The different departments of life are jumbled together— . . . actuated by the demons of profligacy and licentiousness, they are seen everywhere, rambling, riding, rolling, rushing, jostling, mixing, bouncing, cracking, and crashing in one vile ferment of stupidity and corruption." Vauxhall is "without any unity of design, or propriety of disposition." In general, London is a "misshapen and monstrous capital, without head or tail, members or proportion," and only for the benefit of his wards does he deign to "explore the depths of this chaos" (I, 114-17).

3. ALL FIVE major characters are unanimous in their picture of Welsh simplicity, and all five are consistent in their observation of English multiplicity and variety—though each affects a different attitude, determined by his own character. For the young, England seems to offer definite advantages. For the elderly Bramble, it appears at its worst.

Because of Tabby's avarice, Winifred's awe, and Lydia's inexperience, these three seldom offer any direct interpretation of English diversity. Bramble and Jeremy, however, understand it as an effect of increased luxury and commercial progress.

Bramble comments on "the boasted improvements" of Bath. The city is altered since his last visit, yet it has scarcely progressed, since it now reveals "absurdities [which] arise from the general tide of luxury, which hath overspread the nation, and swept away all, even the very dregs of the people" (I, 42-46). Bath is now "a mushroom of opulence," "a mere sink of profligacy and extortion"; its residents are engulfed "by the flood of luxury and extravagance" (I, 73-74). Bramble writes of this "degenerate age, fast sinking into barbarism" (I, 99), and Jeremy too speaks of "the tinsel of the times" (I, 87), noting that even the clergy abounds with "great overgrown dignitaries and rectors, with rubicund noses and gouty ankles, or broad bloated faces, dragging along great swag bellies, the emblems of sloth and indigestion" (I, 94). Here in Bath, Dr. Linden appropriately discourses on "those nations [that] are in a state of nature, undebauched by luxury" (I, 21).

In London Bramble observes those changes which have come about for "the purposes of luxury." He recognizes that "the tide of luxury has swept all the inhabitants from the open country," so that the lowest rural workers are debauched by the opportunity to "live luxuriously." Many factors have contributed to the change, Bramble contends, "but they may be all resolved into the grand source of luxury and corruption" (I, 113-14).

English luxury, corruption, and multiplicity are to be contrasted with the poverty, growth, and simplicity discernible in Scotland, where the expedition heads for the second phase of its tour. Edinburgh and Glasgow are thriving commercial and intellectual centers, but in general the country is not yet fully developed. Jeremy finds Inverary poor, its peasants impoverished. Hunting near Cameron, he is attended by "ragged Highlanders, without shoes or stockings." His landlord's home is "equally rough and hospitable, and savours much of the simplicity of ancient times." Here, "the poems of Ossian are in every mouth," and the "country appears more and more wild and savage" the farther they advance (II, 80-87). He describes the area around Drumlanrig as "one of the wildest tracts in all Scotland" (II, 117).

Friendship and affection are found everywhere in this primitive and impoverished country. Jeremy finds the people "social and attentive in their civilities to strangers" (II, 57). His uncle writes from Edinburgh that "I have met with more kindness, hospitality, and rational entertainment, in a few weeks, than ever I received in any other country during the whole course of my life" (II, 70).

Like his nephew, Bramble emphasizes the poverty and primitivism of the country "generally rough, wild, and mountainous"

(II, 121). He writes from Cameron that "the ground is naturally barren and moorish. The peasants are poorly lodged, meagre in their looks, mean in their apparel, and remarkably dirty" (II, 89). In the Highlands "all is sublimity, silence, and solitude," for "this country is amazingly wild, [and has] . . . a most stupendous appearance of savage nature, with hardly any signs of cultivation, or even of population" (II, 99).

Winifred Jenkins comments on the poverty of "the servants of the country, which are pore drudges, many of them without shoes or stockings" (II, 57). Lydia, true to character, discovers that "the country being exceedingly romantic, suits my turn and inclinations" (II, 106), while her aunt is "inclined to give the whole Scotch nation to the devil, as a pack of insensible brutes, upon whom her accomplishments had been displayed in vain" (II, 112).

Most of the letters written north of the Tweed contain little of the dramatic and much of the didactic—probably because the novelist's enthusiasm for his native country was not to be controlled. Lydia writes only one letter, and Tabby none at all from Scotland. Noticeably, there is small difference between Jeremy's and Bramble's raptures. Since the contrast afforded by divergent perspectives of the English letters is not sustained, and since progression of the five sub-plots is minimal here, letters from Scotland are static. Nevertheless, thematic development is all the more pronounced, as simplicity, primitivism, and social virtues in Scotland are contrasted with variety, luxury, and moral disintegration in England.

Although degeneration is most perceptible in England and primitivism is most perceptible in Scotland, the dualism is never absolute. Distinctions are consistently being drawn in both countries between improvements that result in real progress, and improvements without regard for taste or convenience that result in degeneration.

Architecture at Bath is not wholly objectionable to Bramble. In his opinion "the Square, though irregular, is, on the whole, pretty well laid out, spacious, open, and airy; and . . . by far the most wholesome and agreeable situation in Bath" (I, 43). There are some improvements in London and Westminster, which "are much better paved and lighted than they were formerly. The new streets are spacious, regular, and airy, and the houses generally convenient. The bridge at Blackfriars is a noble monument of taste and public spirit" (I, 112-13). The fortress at Harrowgate "is now converted into a prison, and is the best, in all respects, I ever saw at home or abroad. It stands in a high situation, extremely well ventilated, and has a spacious area within the walls for the health and convenience of all the prisoners" (II, 1).

Art and learning in England are commended when they are not subservient to "the taste and judgment of coffee-house connoisseurs." The landscapes of William Taverner are admired for their magnificence, warmth and organization. "If there is any taste for ingenuity left in a degenerate age, fast sinking into barbarism, this artist, I apprehend, will make a capital figure," Bramble remarks (I, 99). The British Museum is praised for having "a noble collection, and even stupendous" (I, 132). Both Bramble and Jeremy "become members of the Society for the Encouragement of the Arts . . . which will certainly be productive of great advantages to the public, if, from its democratical form, it does not degenerate into cabal and corruption" (I, 151).

Supplementing the praise for improvements in architecture and true learning when they are detected in England are instances of benevolence and friendships developed at English schools. Bramble realizes there is "nothing of equal value with the genuine friendship of a sensible man; a rare jewel!" (I, 48), and he admits that he "should not have been able to stay so long in the place [Bath], if I had not discovered some old friends, whose conversation alleviates my disgust" (I, 70). Despite his general disgust, Bramble must confess that he finds some value in Bath as a meeting place for friends: "I shall leave it with regret; because I must part with some old friends" (I, 98).

Praise of England is more the exception than the rule in these early letters. Disapproval of Scotland, however, not only places this country in a less favorable light than is generally conceded, but frequently enhances the value of England. As Bramble himself acknowledges, comparison with England "is unfavourable to Scotland in all its exteriors, such as, the face of the country in respect to cultivation, the appearance of the bulk of the people, and the language of conversation in general" (II, 71).

Though Scotland is wilder, more savage and primitive than England, there is less cultivation and poorer agriculture. Bramble perceives "that agriculture in this country is not yet brought to that perfection which it has attained in England" (II, 50). The soil at Cameron is "poorly cultivated, and almost altogether unenclosed"; and considering the crop of oats and barley, Bramble admits that "the first are much better, the last much worse, than those of the same species in England" (II, 88-92). There is an air of state and grandeur about Scottish villas, but "their gardens and parks are not comparable to those of England" (II, 75).

People in Scotland are more friendly, more hospitable, and more honest, yet they live in greater filth and poverty than the English. An inn at Edinburgh is "filthy and disagreeable in all respects" (II, 49); "impurities are discharged upon the streets from Edinburgh windows every night" (II, 53); the peasants around Cameron are "remarkably dirty" (II, 89); and it is generally conceded that "the peasantry of Scotland are certainly on a poor footing all over the kingdom" (II, 120).

Progress in England has resulted in greater amusements and diversions, a more refined language, improved agriculture, greater wealth and commerce—but it has also resulted in disorder: social, economic, political, esthetic, and moral. Primitivism in Scotland reveals simplicity, integrity, and true affection—but it also reveals filth, poverty, and an undeveloped agriculture. Thematically, Smollett is posing the same kind of cultural relativism that the Scottish critics and historians employed in examining and evaluating "the noble savage": as he is found in America and in Africa, as he is revealed in the poems of Ossian and of Homer. For Smollett, as for Ferguson, Kames and Robertson, neither primitivism nor the idea of progress is wholly tenable, for each has its virtues and defects.

Several factors contribute to the illusion that Smollett is pre-
senting an indiscriminate condemnation of "progress" and an un-
swerving approbation of "primitivism." One is the harshness of
Bramble's censure of England; however, this is somewhat offset by
Lydia's and Jeremy's approval of England, and by the knowledge
that Bramble's criticism is partially the result of an over-active
spleen. Second, much of the praise for "progress" is buried within
the tedious Scottish letters, where it is only tangential to the materials on hand. Finally, there is the obviously sympathetic portrayal of two subsidiary characters, Humphry Clinker and Obadiah
Lismahago, both of whom are more closely allied with the simplicity of Scotland than with the degeneration of England.

4. OBADIAH LISMAHAGO, the disputatious Caledonian,
who first meets the travelers just before their entry into Scotland,
becomes part of the expedition when the group returns to England
some weeks later. A veteran of foreign wars, Lismahago has spent
most of his life among the primitive Indians in America. Essential
to Lismahago's character is his love for polemics; "he is so addicted
to wrangling, that he will cavil at the clearest truths, and, in the
pride of argumentation, attempt to reconcile contradictions" (II,
16).

Though Lismahago is generally seen as Smollett's principal
spokesman for the merits of Scotland, his role in the novel scarcely
sustains this view. His argumentative manner and his consistent
"attempt to reconcile contradictions" make him an ardent spokesman for cultural relativity: for the virtues of primitivism and the
idea of progress, and against their defects.

In his first appearance, prior to the departure of the expedition
to Scotland, Lismahago's conversations are primarily concerned
with the American Indians. The discussion of his marriage to the
squaw Squinkinacoosta leads Tabitha to inquire about the wed-
ding dress of his bride: "whether she wore high-breasted stays or
bodice, a robe of silk or velvet, and laces of Mechlin or minionete—

she supposed, as they were connected with the French, she used *rouge*, and had her hair dressed in the Parisian fashion." Tabby's questions are understandable, considering the weeks she has spent in London and the fashionable resorts of England. Lismahago, however, declines to satisfy her curiosity, and counters, "Neither the simplicity of their manners, nor the commerce of their country, would admit of those articles of luxury which are deemed magnificence in Europe . . . they were too virtuous and sensible to encourage the introduction of any fashion which might help to render them corrupt and effeminate." Tabby inquires about religion, "whither his consort had been High Church or Low Church, Presbyterian, or Anabaptist, or had been favoured with any glimmering of the new light of the gospel?" As with the matter of dress, Lismahago replies that "religion . . . is among those Indians a matter of great simplicity—they never heard of any *alliance between Church and State*" (II, 21-23). Suitably, when the conversation turns to a consideration of language, Lismahago employs the same standards of judgment. The analogy between the American Indians and the Scots is not made directly, but the implied comparison between these two kinds of primitivism is too strong to be denied, for Lismahago insists that the Scots "retain the ancient language" with its purity and simplicity, whereas "the modern English, from affectation and false refinement, had weakened, and even corrupted their language" (II, 28).

Appearing as he does, immediately prior to the entry of the expedition into Scotland, Lismahago serves as a brief prolegomenon for men and manners to be encountered. Once the group leaves Scotland, however, Lismahago appropriately reappears. Argumentative by nature, he objects to unqualified praise for primitivistic Scotland, just as he objects to unqualified praise for England. While seeming to favor his native country, Lismahago is by no means a Scottish enthusiast. By shifting the emphasis to morality, Lismahago insists on an examination of England and Scotland on the basis of their mutual virtues and vices.

Thus, commended for signs of diminishing poverty in his

native Scotland, Lismahago counters with a diatribe against wealth wherever it is found:

> Those who reproach a nation for its poverty, when it is not owing to the profligacy or vice of the people, deserve no answer. The Lacedemonians were poorer than the Scotch, when they took the lead among all the free states of Greece, and were esteemed above them all for their valour and their virtue. The most respectable heroes of ancient Rome, such as Fabricius, Cincinnatus, and Regulus, were poorer than the poorest freeholder in Scotland . . . and poverty was so far from being a reproach, that it added fresh laurels to her fame, because it indicated a noble contempt of wealth, which was proof against all the arts of corruption.   (II, 129-30)

Although Lismahago admits that his country is much improved since its union with England, he insists on distinguishing between "the natural progress of improvement" and changes wrought by "luxury" (II, 131-34):

> Woe be to that nation where the multitude is at liberty to follow their own inclinations! Commerce is undoubtedly a blessing, while restrained within its proper channels; but a glut of wealth brings along with it a glut of evils. It brings false taste, false appetite, false wants, profusion, venality, contempt of order, engendering a spirit of licentiousness, insolence, and faction, that keeps the community in continual ferment, and in time destroys all the distinctions of civil society; so that universal anarchy and uproar must ensue. Will any sensible man affirm, that the national advantages of opulence are to be sought on these terms? No, sure;—but I am one of those who think, that, by proper regulations, commerce may produce every national benefit, without the allay of such concomitant evils.   (II, 136)

To see Lismahago as the fulfillment of Smollett's intent, his "purpose in the novel as a whole: to decry the English and exalt the Scots," as one critic has done,[12] is to distort the essence of Lismahago's dialectic, which reinforces thematic development in the novel. With Lismahago, as eventually with Bramble and the expedition as a whole, there is never a clear-cut opposition between England and Scotland. Variety and simplicity, wealth and poverty,

Matt Bramble - health, mind, body, Soul
Tabitha Bramble- husband.
Lydia Melford - search for wilson
Humphry Clinkles - search for position in
life
Jeremy melford- understand life

pg. 13
Lydia

Jeremy
13

progress and primitivism—these assume meaning relative only to his moral perspective. And for Lismahago, rather, the real contraries are growth and corruption, integrity and dishonesty, virtue and vice.

5. INSTRUMENTAL in the development of plot, but also in the unfolding of the didactic theme which reconciles primitivism with the idea of progress, is Humphry Clinker, the impoverished footman who joins the expedition between Bath and London and remains with the group during the entire tour. Clinker, like Lismahago, is not a letter-writer, but he provides a significant influence upon the five central characters in the novel.

"So far as I can observe, the fellow's character is downright simplicity, warmed with a kind of enthusiasm, which renders him very susceptible of gratitude and attachment to his benefactors," Matthew Bramble writes from London about his new footman (I, 201). Bramble is "pleased with the gratitude of Clinker, as well as with the simplicity of his character" (I, 108), when the man states his determination to serve him all his life without fee or reward. When Clinker is arrested as a highwayman, the spectators detect a villainy in his aspect, whereas Bramble knows he is "the very picture of simplicity" (I, 190). At times the squire is amused "at the poor fellow's simplicity" (I, 181). But he also finds himself "a sufferer by his simplicity," particularly when "in great simplicity of heart" (II, 7-8) Clinker hauls his nude master ashore while bathing, in the belief that he is drowning.

Jeremy's new valet is noticeably "the very contrast of Humphry Clinker" (I, 201). Jeremy observes that "Humphry may be compared to an English pudding, composed of good wholesome flour and suet, and Dutton to a syllabub or iced froth, which, though agreeable to the taste, has nothing solid or substantial" (II, 40). Dutton "takes snuff *à la mode de France*, but values himself chiefly upon his skill and dexterity in hairdressing" (I, 201). He "wears a solitaire, uses paint, and takes rappee with all the grimace of a

French marquis"; for traveling he has "a riding dress, jack-boots, leather breeches, a scarlet waistcoat with gold binding, a laced hat, a hanger, a French posting whip in his hand, and his hair *en queue*" (I, 206). He dazzles Winifred Jenkins with his finery, and accompanies her to a play while "dressed in a silk coat, made at Paris for his former master, with a tawdry waistcoat of tarnished brocade" (II, 41).

This contrast between Dutton's foppery and Clinker's semi-nudity is integral to the theme of primitivism and progress in the novel. When Clinker first joins the expedition, Tabitha calls him "a beggarly rascal, that . . . had ne'er a shirt to his back; and had the impudence to shock her sight by showing his posteriors." Win Jenkins confirms her assertion "with respect to his nakedness, observing, at the same time, that he had a skin as fair as alabaster"; and Jeremy writes that "the rags that he wore could hardly conceal what decency requires to be covered." Clinker insists he is merely the victim of chance, for his breeches cracked behind *after* he got into the saddle; nevertheless, he offers by way of explanation: "I'm a poor Wiltshire lad. I ha'n't a shirt in the world that I can call my own, nor a rag of clothes, an' please your ladyship, but what you see—I have no friend nor relation upon earth to help me out." With Bramble's aid, Clinker retrieves some of his own clothes from pawn, but he has difficulty appeasing Tabby, "who had not yet digested the affront of his naked skin" (I, 105-08). The kindly Winifred is scarcely offended, for she knows that "Umphry Klinker, [is] a good sole as ever broke bread; which shows that a scalded cat may pruve a good mouser, and a hound be stanch, thof he has got narro hare on his buttocks" (I, 140-41). Jeremy suspects that Win has been attracted to Clinker's merits, "ever since he exhibited the pattern of his naked skin" (II, 40); and in Glasgow Win even finds an old witch who tells her many things, "descriving Mr. Clinker to a hair" (II, 110). Clinker himself tells the squire that he has been "a poor bankrupt from the beginning. Your honour's goodness found me when I was—naked—when I was—sick and forlorn" (II, 184).

Ultimately, it is discovered that Clinker is the bastard son of

Bramble, whom he has always sought under the name of "Lloyd." His new-found father, therefore, recognizes that he himself is responsible for his son's poverty, his nudity and hunger, for "in consequence of my changing my name, and going abroad . . . thy poor mother and thou have been left to want and misery. I am really shocked at the consequence of my own folly" (II, 187).

The name Humphry Clinker has assumed since childhood is itself indicative of the lamentable condition in which Bramble has found him. His praenomen is obviously derived from the common seventeenth- and eighteenth-century phrase, *to dine with Duke Humphry*, which implied going dinnerless. It is a phrase appearing in Smollett's *Roderick Random* (ch. LV); but also it is crucial to a review of *Humphry Clinker*, printed in the *Universal Magazine* (XLIX, 1771, 256-57), where a critic, commenting on the sparseness of entertainment in the novel, suggests that "the book might as well have been intitled The Feast of Duke Humphry." The variant meanings which Dr. Johnson's *Dictionary* lists for *clinker* make it possible that the term refers to the fetters Humphry wears in prison, when he is arrested as a highwayman; though an alternate scatological meaning in Farmer and Henly appears to link the name with the nudity surrounding Clinker in the novel, and is conceivably more indicative of the general fetters of poverty, hunger and bastardy which he has worn all his life.[13]

The contrast between nudity (occasioned by poverty, and indicative of primitivism) and clothes (occasioned by luxury, and indicative of progress) forms a central motif in the novel. Though the motif is most apparent in an examination of Humphry Clinker, it is by no means restricted to his person.

The opening letter from Matt Bramble sounds the first note of this motif when Dr. Lewis, the squire's correspondent in Wales, is advised to "let Morgan's widow have . . . forty shillings to clothe her children" (I, 6). In contrast with her brother's altruism which clothes the naked, Tabitha's vanity, revealed in the letter immediately following, demands that her housekeeper in Wales send

> without loss of time, the following articles, viz. my rose-collard
> neglejay, with green robins, my yellow damask, and my black velvet
> suit, with the short hoop; my bloo quilted petticoat, my green man-
> teel, my laced apron, my French commode, Macklin head and lap-
> pets, and the litel box with my jowls. (I, 6)

When the squire gives twenty pounds to an impoverished woman
and her dying child, Tabitha indignantly insists that "charity begins
at home. Twenty pounds would buy me a complete suit of flowered
silk, trimmings and all" (I, 28). From Bath, Tabby sends for her
"riding habit, hat, and feather," and simultaneously expresses her
indignation at her brother, who "would give away the shirt off his
back" (I, 56-57). Significantly, it is Tabby who raises the most
strenuous objections to Clinker's semi-nudity, from which she
deduces his villainous character. Within two weeks of Clinker's
appearance, Jeremy notes a change in his aunt:

> Mrs. Tabitha declared he [Clinker] was a sober, civilised fellow, very
> respectful, and very industrious, and, she believed, a good Christian
> into the bargain. One would think Clinker must really have some
> very extraordinary talent to ingratiate himself in this manner with a
> virago of her character, so fortified against him with prejudice and
> resentment; but the truth is, since the adventure of Salthill, Mrs.
> Tabby seems to be entirely changed. She has left off scolding the
> servants, an exercise which was grown habitual, and even seemed
> necessary to her constitution. . . . (I, 131)

This alteration is confirmed by Bramble, who writes from London
that "Tabby is a changed creature" (I, 140). Clinker's religious
enthusiasm is clearly instrumental in changing Tabitha. Before
long, the avaricious spinster is attending Methodist prayer meetings,
listening to sermons, singing hymns—all through the promptings
of her inspired footman. Tabby's first letter from London is a strange
amalgam of avarice and religious homilies. Soon, there are times
when "even Tabitha's charity was awakened," and when "even
Tabby's heart was melted" (II, 10-14). The change in Tabby,
which Clinker initiates, is sustained in the final section of the novel

through Obadiah Lismahago, who inhibits the avarice and the vain emphasis upon clothes, and helps develop her altruism and simple affections.

The clothes-motif is perceptible in Winifred Jenkins, and Clinker has a pervasive influence upon her soul also. From the beginning, Win alternates between benevolence and vanity. Appalled at the "dressing, and fiddling, and dancing" at Bath, she is nevertheless enchanted with her "yellow trolopea":

> Mrs. Drab, the manty-maker, says [it] will look very well when it is scowred and smoaked with silfur—You knows as how yellow fitts my fizzogmony. God he knows what havoc I shall make among the mail sex, when I make my first appearance in this killing collar, with a full suit of gaze, as good as new, that I bought last Friday, of Madam Friponeau, the French mullaner. (I, 53-54)

By the time she gets to London, she has her "hair cut and pippered, and singed, and bolstered, and buckled in the newest fashion, by a French freezer. . . . I now carries my head higher than arrow private gentlewoman of Vales." At the same time, though, as an obvious result of Clinker's Methodism, she disdainfully announces that "the pleasures of London are no better than sower whey and stale cyder, when compared to the joys of the New Gerusalem" (I, 142). She sends her friend Mary Jones "as a token, a turkey-shell comb, a kiple of yards of green ribbon"; but she also forwards "a sarment upon the nothingness of good works, which was preached in the Tabernacle" (I, 202). Jeremy writes that Winifred follows her mistress's system of devotion implicitly: "This, indeed, she found the more agreeable, as it was in a great measure introduced and confirmed by the ministry of Clinker, with whose personal merit she seems to have been struck ever since he exhibited the pattern of his naked skin . . ." (II, 40). In Edinburgh Winifred recognizes that "Sattin has had power to temp me in the shape of van Ditton, the young squire's wally-de-shamble; but by God's grease he did not purvail" (II, 55). As a result, she concentrates solely upon the heart of Clinker, whom she eventually wins, once vanity is on the wane.

On three occasions the theme of nudity is identified with Winifred. In Bath she is thrown into a "gumbustion" when she drops her petticoat, but then, as she observes, "what did that signify? —they mought laff, but they could see nothing; for I was up to the sin in water" (I, 55). In Scarborough, a fire at the inn prompts Win to throw herself from the window: "This maiden was just as she had started out of bed; the moon shone very bright, and a fresh breeze of wind blowing, none of Mrs. Winifred's beauties could possibly escape the view of the fortunate Clinker, whose heart was not able to withstand the united force of so many charms" (I, 230). On a third occasion, just before the expedition leaves Scotland, Winifred is seen again in all her natural simplicity:

> I went in the morning to a private place, along with the housemaid, and we bathed in our birth-day soot, after the fashion of the country; and behold, whilst we dabbled in the loff, Sir George Coon started up with a gun; but we clapt our hands to our faces, and passed by him to the place where we had left our smocks. . . . My comfit is, he knew not which was which; and, as the saying is, *all cats in the dark are grey.* (II, 111)

Alternating between frivolous clothes and nudity, Win Jenkins partakes of the avarice of Tabitha who is consistently identified with clothes, but she also partakes of the simplicity of Clinker who is consistently identified with nudity. Obadiah Lismahago, the bitter antagonist of luxury and corruption, is seen once with "his long lank limbs and posteriors exposed to the wind" (II, 162); and even Matthew Bramble is seen "naked on the beach" at Scarborough (II, 8). Although the reviewer for *Gentleman's Magazine* in 1771, like many critics afterward, severely reprimands Smollett for his "stercoraceous" and "prurient" style, he is obviously overlooking the relationship between nudity and clothes, a motif central to the major theme of primitivism and the idea of progress. Living luxuriously and wearing fine clothes is a symbol of moral and social disintegration in England; living simply and with poor apparel is a symbol of the kindness, hospitality, and moral integrity in Scotland. In the same respect, clothes are symbolic of moral degeneration in individual characters, and nudity becomes symbolic either of their virtue or of their regeneration.

The persistent contrast between nakedness and clothes in Smollett's novel is not too remote from the clothes-symbolism in *King Lear*, where the recognition that "unaccomodated man is no more but . . . a poor, bare, forked animal" leads to Lear's tearing off his unnatural trappings and reverting, like Tom, to a naked, bestial, unsophisticated state, at one with the elements. It is similar to Swift's satiric portrayal in *A Tale of a Tub*, where worshippers of the tailor-deity conclude that "man himself [is] but a micro-coat . . . religion a cloak, honesty a pair of shoes worn out in the dirt, self-love a surtout, vanity a shirt, and conscience a pair of breeches, which, though a cover for lewdness as well as nastiness, is easily slipt down for the service of both." And it finds a parallel in Carlyle's *Sartor Resartus*, where the editor of Teufelsdröckh's manuscript descants on those "broken-winged thinkers . . . regarding Clothes as a property, not an accident, as quite natural and spontaneous, like the leaves of trees, like the plummage of birds." Smollett—like Shakespeare, Swift, and Carlyle—is insistent upon the superfluity of man's external wrappings. Clothes are indicative of the breakdown of natural order in Shakespeare, of religious order in Swift, of spiritual order in Carlyle. In Smollett, however, clothes in their excess are indicative of social and economic chaos, and of the moral disintegration induced by opulence, luxury, and the degeneration which is mistaken for "progress."

6. ALTHOUGH the tour itself is divisible into three major parts, organization in *Humphry Clinker* is more dependent upon theme than upon plot. The entire expedition lasts some eight months, from early April until late November. The first part, ex-

tending to Jeremy's letter of July 10 from Newcastle-upon-Tyne, presents the five main characters with a picture of progress and variety in England. Part two, extending to Bramble's letter of September 20 (from Buxton?), provides the protagonists with a view of the greater primitivism and simplicity in Scotland. The letters which describe the two meetings with Lismahago form an integral part of this second section, even though they emanate from England, since they focus upon the tour of Scotland. Thematically, each of the five characters is faced with a moral choice after departure from Scotland. Reconciliation of these seemingly antithetical ways of life, as symbolized by England and by Scotland, becomes the problem in the final section of the novel, as the expedition descends homeward to Wales. Here, sub-plots are fully developed and given their larger meanings, relative to the central didactic theme.

Letters from the return trip down the western coast of England are perceptibly different from the previous English and Scottish epistles. Materials of travel are discarded in this final section. Topography is abandoned as a unifying device. We are no longer confronted with descriptive scenery or introduced to new customs and manners. Not one of the eighteen letters in this final section bears any indication of the place from which it has been sent.

Earlier, the five major characters were offered the terms of the contraries represented by the two countries they visited; now, on their return trip, they face a choice. Significantly, the choice is not between England and Scotland, but between virtues and vices found in both places. Thus, neither the "progress" of England nor the "primitivism" of Scotland is emphasized, but rather those aspects of both progress and primitivism which can contribute to man's happiness. This choice has been adequately prepared for by the relativity of views offered throughout; by the progressive development of virtues in Tabitha and Winifred; by the partial and relative praise of England and censure of Scotland by Bramble and Jeremy; and by Lismahago's constant "attempt to reconcile contradictions" (II, 16).

The travelers make four principal stops on their return journey, when they visit with Lord Oxmington, Mr. Baynard, Sir Thomas Bulford and Charles Dennison.

Contrasting with the warmth and affection the group has just encountered in Scotland, Lord Oxmington is "more remarkable for his pride and caprice than for his hospitality and understanding." With Oxmington there is "much state" but "no courtesy" (II, 138). At Sir Thomas Bulford's estate there is much warmth and hospitality, but little taste and discretion, so that all the guests suffer by Sir Thomas' constant search for amusement (II, 159 ff.).

With Mr. Baynard, on the other hand, Matt Bramble finds that everything is "cold, comfortless, and disgusting, except the looks of my friend Baynard, which declared the warmth of his affection and humanity." Though Baynard has maintained an ideal of true rural felicity from the beginning, he has reckoned without the vanity of his wife, who is "excited by show and ostentation" and demands "all the superfluities of pomp and pageantry." She has succeeded in turning his estate into "a naked circus of loose sand" with her attempts at improvement, so that Baynard himself is "hurried about in a perpetual tumult, amidst a mob of beings pleased with rattles, baubles, and gewgaws" (II, 143-59).

Not until he visits Charles Dennison, his old university friend, does Bramble encounter "that pitch of rural felicity at which I have been aspiring these twenty years in vain." Both Dennison and his wife are in no fear of leading a life of dissipation and extravagance, which they equally detest. Instead, they hold in view certain objectives—"health of body, peace of mind, and the private satisfaction of domestic quiet, unallayed by actual want, and uninterrupted by the fears of indigence." While living in the country, Dennison has effected "a considerable saving on the side of dress, in being delivered from the oppressive imposition of ridiculous modes invented by ignorance and adopted by folly." As Dennison himself points out, he has not been at the mercy of "pride, envy, and ambition. . . . Those, in times of luxury and dissipation, are the rocks upon which all the small estates in the country are wrecked" (II, 190-200).

Dennison's son, George, proves to be "Wilson" the actor, whose love-affair with Lydia has formed one of the sub-plots in the novel. Since Lydia has already decided that she is "heartily tired of this itinerant way of life" and "quite dizzy with a perpetual succession of objects," she is quite prepared for marriage with George and a life on the Dennison estate in England, where prosperity can be attained without luxury, and simplicity without poverty. She writes to her "dear Letty":

> Nature never intended me for the busy world; I long for repose and solitude, where I can enjoy that disinterested friendship which is not to be found among crowds, and indulge those pleasing reveries that shun the hurry and tumult of fashionable society. Unexperienced as I am in the commerce of life, I have seen enough to give me a disgust to the generality of those who carry it on.   (II, 173)

Jeremy also seems prepared to moderate his search for diversions. Chagrined at his impassioned hostility to "Wilson the actor," whose outer garments had led him to misjudge a man "worthy of friendship and esteem," Jery now proposes his former antagonist as "a model for imitation." He writes to his friend at Oxford about the lesson he has learned:

> I am . . . mortified to reflect what flagrant injustice we every day commit, and what absurd judgment we form, in viewing objects through the falsifying medium of prejudice and passion. Had you asked me a few days ago the picture of Wilson the player, I should have drawn a portrait very unlike the real person and character of George Dennison. Without all doubt, the greatest advantage acquired in travelling and perusing mankind in the original, is that of dispelling those shameful clouds that darken the faculties of the mind, preventing it from judging with candour and precision.
> (II, 206)

Jeremy considers that if Mr. Dennison had a daughter, he might be tempted to join their rural joys. Indeed, once Lydia's boarding-school friend arrives for the marriage, her charms provoke some idle reflections about the fulfillment of his destiny.

While Lydia and Jeremy are considering the need for simplicity and order, and preparing to temper their fondness for variety, Matt Bramble is becoming cognizant of his own need for variety and change:

> I begin to think I have put myself on the superannuated list too soon, and absurdly sought for health in the retreats of laziness. I am persuaded, that all valetudinarians are too sedentary, too regular, and too cautious. We should sometimes increase the motion of the machine, to *unclog the wheels of life*; and now and then take a plunge amidst the waves of excess, in order to case-harden the constitution. I have even found a change of company as necessary as a change of air, to promote a vigorous circulation of the spirits, which is the very essence and criterion of good health. (II, 215-16)

As a result, Bramble changes his role as spectator to that of participant, for he intends "to renounce all sedentary amusements" (II, 231). Coming to the aid of Baynard, whose wife has fortunately seen fit to relieve him by her death, Bramble and Mr. Dennison undertake the task of reconstructing the disintegrated estate. They bring to it improvements which reflect taste, convenience, and economy, without the superfluities of ostentation and pomp that can only result in barbarism and chaos.

Tabitha also changes, curbing her avarice and vanity, and appearing quite social and benevolent. Her nephew observes that since arrangements for her marriage with Lismahago, "the vinegar of Mrs. Tabby is remarkably dulcified" (II, 207). The reader knows Jeremy's observation is a valid one, for Tabby's final letter is addressed, with some mark of affection for the first time, to "Good Mrs. Gwyllim," and signed "Your loving friend" (II, 231-32). Once Lismahago removes her bridal "mantle of green velvet laced with gold" and exchanges it for "a fur cloak of American sables" (II, 226)—a symbolic gesture, related to the clothes-motif—Tabitha replaces ostentation with simplicity, and selfishness with sociability.

A change is also manifest in Winifred Jenkins in this final section of the novel, for her marriage to Humphry Clinker (now, as Bramble's son, called "Matthew Lloyd") raises them in station and in dress. Winifred writes with no small pride that her Mr. Lloyd "is now out of livery, and wares ruffles; but I new him when he was out at elbows, and had not a rag to kiver his pistereroes" (II, 213), and her final letter revels in "being, by God's blessing, removed to a higher spear." Just as Mrs. Lismahago must recognize the need for more affection and benevolence with the servants, Mrs. Lloyd must recognize the need for less. "You'll excuse my being familiar with the lower sarvants of the family," she writes now to Mrs. Jones (formerly addressed as "Dear Molly"), as she urges her to "behave respectful, and keep a proper distance" (II, 233).

REFERENCES

1. Samuel Johnson, *A Journey to the Western Islands of Scotland*, ed. R. W. Chapman (Oxford, 1924), p. 12.

2. James Boswell, *The Journal of a Tour to the Hebrides*, ed. R. W. Chapman (Oxford, 1924), p. 167.

3. Louis L. Martz, *The Later Career of Tobias Smollett* (New Haven, 1942) p. 125, finds in *Humphry Clinker* "essential kinship with Smollett's *Present State* and its many predecessors under that title." He points to extracts from Bramble's letter of April 23, printed in the *Whitehall Evening-Post* under title of "The Present State of Bath," and Bramble's letter of May 29, printed under title of "The Present State of London," *Whitehall Evening-Post*, June 15-18, 1771, pp. 18-20.

4. Horace Walpole, *Memoirs of the Reign of King George the Third* (London, 1894), IV, 218.

5. Martz, pp. 68, 170.

6. James R. Foster suggests in "Smollett and *The Atom*," *PMLA*, LXVIII (1953), 1032-46, that ". . . enough presumptive evidence can be found to show that there is much in the traditional view of Smollett's authorship to recommend it." Though Foster argues persuasively, still, it is only "presumptive evidence" which

leads to his conclusion that ". . . until someone comes forward with reputable proof to the contrary, it seems reasonably safe to conclude that Dr. Smollett was our author." It is indeed *possible* that Smollett wrote *The Atom,* and Dr. Foster certainly sustains that possibility. But it is hardly "reasonably safe" to contend that Smollett *must* have written the book. Lewis M. Knapp's earlier assessment of the problem seems much more "reasonably safe" and judicious: ". . . we lack the external evidence necessary to prove conclusively that he wrote it" (*Tobias Smollett* [Princeton, 1949], pp. 281-83).

7. Lois Whitney, *Primitivism and the Idea of Progress* (Baltimore, 1934), pp. 42-51.

8. F. B. Kaye, ed. *Mandeville's The Fable of the Bees* (Oxford, 1924), I, xciv-ciii; Whitney, p. xiii; Ronald S. Crane, "Anglican Apologetics and the Idea of Progress, 1699-1745," MP, XXXI (1934), 273-306, 349-82; Margaret M. Fitzgerald, *First Follow Nature* (New York, 1947), pp. 1-197; Alan Dugald McKillop, *The Background of Thomson's Seasons* (Minneapolis, 1942), p. 89.

9. Adam Ferguson, *An Essay on the History of Civil Society* (London, 1773), pp. 410-17.

10. William Robertson, *The History of America* (London, 1821), I, 321-22, 342-43; II, 89-108.

11. Henry Home, Lord Kames, *Sketches of the History of Man* (Edinburgh, 1778), II, 125-42, 201-02, 296.

12. Martz, p. 170.

13. John S. Farmer and W. E. Henley, *Slang and its Analogues* (London, 1891), II, 125.

CHAPTER SEVEN. *CONCLUSIONS*

RURAL FELICITY, the ideal toward which each of the characters in *Humphry Clinker* seems to be striving by the close of the novel, embodies a way of life, as far removed from the "primitivism" discerned in the Scottish Highlands as from the "progress" encountered at Bath and London. It appears rather to encompass the virtues of both and the vices of neither: wealth without ostentation, simplicity without poverty. Indeed, this bucolic existence, anticipating a congruity of basic oppositions, is not too remote from the way of life which Roderick anticipates with Narcissa, Peregrine with Emilia, Renaldo with Monimia, and Launcelot with Aurelia. Like the culmination of each of Smollett's novels, *The Expedition of Humphry Clinker* closes within sight of happiness, that great concern of the eighteenth century.

Earlier in the period, Alexander Pope also concerned himself with happiness. But in *An Essay on Man* happiness, "our being's end and aim," consisted in conformity to universal order, resignation within the largely invisible scheme of Providence. True knowledge, dependent upon the recognition that whatever is—in this great chain of being—is right, is opposed by pride, aspiring beyond the law of sufficient reason and pre-established harmony. Pride is at once a threat to happiness and the cause for suffering.

Pope's universe, reinforcing the mathematics of Newton, the metaphysics of Leibniz, and the geological theology of Bishop Burnet, was scarcely a new concept for the eighteenth century. Pope simply became its outstanding spokesman. When Defoe precipitates Robinson Crusoe into a series of adventures, designed to illustrate the sagacity of his father's advice that he ought not to aspire to a fortune and position beyond the station into which he has been born, Defoe is clearly operating within the assumptions basic to Pope's universe. Only when he is isolated from society on the island does Crusoe recognize the extent of his own pride, the sagacity of his father, and the greater wisdom of knowing one's place in the divine order.

How remote is Pope's static and mechanical universe—expressed in his own balanced couplets, no less than in the symmetrical gardens at Versailles, the proportioned music of Mozart, the geometric propositions of Spinoza—from the kind of world which the "romantics" were envisioning before too many decades! Before long, Pope's static chain has been transformed into a hierarchical ladder, up which the aspiring soul is encouraged to climb in achieving significances and values.

Keats envisions such a ladder in *Endymion*, where Peona is asked, "Wherein lies happiness?" It is found only at the tip-top of this ladder, composed of entanglements increasingly rich, she is assured. By degrees we can ascend to the chief intensity, love, in our arduous pursuit of the essence of experience, the things of beauty that are forever a joy. Keats' empirical pursuit is not too remote from that which Shelley delineates, or which John Stuart Mill gleaned in his reading of Wordsworth during that autumn of 1828, recorded in his *Autobiography*. There is "real, permanent happiness in tranquil contemplation," in states of feeling and sensation, in love and sympathy; Mill detects this in Wordsworth and in "the anti-selfconsciousness theory of Carlyle." This is a happiness that cannot be gained from reasoned analysis and the ordering of outward circumstance.

But for Smollett, happiness is not to be confused with Pope's assumptions about an orderly and rational universe, no more than it can be identified with Keats' empirical pursuit of the things of beauty. With Smollett, as with the Scottish Common-Sense School, it is to be discerned in things, no less than in their order; in sensation, no less than in reason; and in unity, no less than in multiplicity and variety.

"What, then, is that mysterious thing called *Happiness*, which may have place in such a variety of stations, and to which circumstances in one age or nation thought necessary, are in another held to be destructive or of no effect?" asks Adam Ferguson in the eighth section (Part One) of *An Essay on the History of Civil Society*. "If the preceding observations on this subject be just, it arises more from the pursuit, than from the attainment of any end whatever; and in every new situation to which we arrive, even in the course of a prosperous life, it depends more on the degree in which our minds are properly employed, than it does on the circumstances in which we are destined to act, on the materials which are placed in our hands, or the tools with which we are furnished."

With Ferguson, as with Smollett, happiness is dependent upon "the degree in which our minds are properly employed." Not to be found in any particular end, happiness resides rather in the moral and virtuous manner through which we pursue our goals. It lies no more in reason than in the passions, but emerges from a basic harmony of the two, as Roderick Random discerns at the close of his adventures, when virtue and philosophy begin governing the unruly passions, and the impetuous transports of those passions can be channeled toward the tranquility of a love for Narcissa. It is the consequence of the congruity of judgment and imagination, as Peregrine Pickle learns, for happiness with Emilia can be reached only after his judgment has contained the bold sallies and wild extravagances of his fertile fancy. It results from the proper balance of nature and art, both encouraged to moderate their demands within civil society, as Renaldo and Count Fathom are taught in their search for happiness. And it is to be found through the gratification of selfish desires, no less than through the gratification of social and benevolent feelings, as Launcelot Greaves comes to recognize before the close of his experiences.

In his persistent reconciliation of these major contradictions, Smollett is unmistakably offering a panacea to the vices and follies of his age, and fulfilling intentions disclosed in his prefaces to *Roderick Random* and *Ferdinand Count Fathom*. Folly is the greatest deterrent to happiness in the novels. And the greatest folly for Smollett, the consistent butt of his satire, lies in the position assumed by extremists, divided into opposing camps and quarreling, like the Hobbesian and the Shaftesburian, about issues more imaginary than real.

The novelist certainly emerges from this faction as a figure who is neither ambiguous nor contradictory. And he is hardly the superficial humorist portrayed by most critics for the past century-and-a-half. A well-integrated representative of eighteenth-century thought, Smollett is never an exponent of scientific realism and mechanism, emanating out of Hobbes and Locke; nor is he an adherent to the rational idealism which maintained an unwavering belief in man's reason and self-determination, as it developed out of the Cambridge Platonists. Smollett, rather, is representative of a third and influential, though much neglected movement, the Scottish Common-Sense School, which devoted itself to bridging the gap between the major oppositions of the century.

A SELECTED BIBLIOGRAPHY

I. TOBIAS SMOLLETT

PRIMARY SOURCES:

Smollett, Tobias. *A Compleat History of England, Deduced from the Descent of Julius Caesar to the Treaty of Aix-la-Chapelle.* 4 vols. London, 1757-58.

——. *A Compendium of Authentic and Entertaining Voyages, digested in Chronological Series.* 7 vols. London, 1766.

——. *An Essay on the External Use of Water,* ed. Claude E. Jones. Baltimore, 1935.

——. *The History of England from the Revolution to the Death of George II.* 4 vols. London, 1841.

——. *The Letters of Tobias Smollett,* ed. Edward S. Noyes. Cambridge, Mass., 1926.

——. "New Smollett Letters," ed. Henry W. Meikle, in *The Times Literary Supplement.* London, July 24, 31, 1943.

——. *The Present State of All Nations, containing a Geographical, Natural, Commercial, and Political History of all the Countries in the Known World.* 8 vols. London, 1768-69.

——. *Travels through France and Italy,* ed. Thomas Seccombe. London, 1919.

——. *The Works of Tobias Smollett,* ed. George Saintsbury. 12 vols. London, n.d.

SECONDARY SOURCES:

Baker, Ernest A. *The History of the English Novel.* 10 vols. London, 1924-39.

Boege, F. W. *Smollett's Reputation as a Novelist.* Princeton, N. J., 1947.

Brander, Laurence. *Tobias Smollett.* Colchester, 1951.

Buck, Howard Swazey. *A Study in Smollett, chiefly "Peregrine Pickle."* New Haven, Conn., 1925.

Foster, James R. *History of the Pre-Romantic Novel in England.* New York, 1949.

Hazlitt, William. *Lectures on the Comic Writers,* in P. P. Howe's Centenary Edition of *The Complete Works of William Hazlitt.* London, 1931.

Joliat, Eugene. *Smollett et la France.* Paris, 1935.

Jones, Claude E. *Smollett Studies.* Berkeley, 1942.

Kahrl, George Morrow. *Tobias Smollett, Traveler-Novelist.* Chicago, 1945.

Knapp, Lewis Mansfield. *Tobias Smollett, Doctor of Men and Manners.* Princeton, N. J., 1949.

Martz, Louis L. *The Later Career of Tobias Smollett.* New Haven, Conn., 1942.

McKillop, Alan Dugald. *The Early Masters of English Fiction.* Lawrence, Kansas, 1956.

Putney, Rufus D. "The Plan of Peregrine Pickle," *PMLA,* LX (1945), 1051-65.

Scott, Walter. *Lives of Eminent Novelists and Dramatists.* London, n.d.

Whitridge, Arnold. *Tobias Smollett.* n.p., 1925.

II. THE SCOTTISH WRITERS

PRIMARY SOURCES:

Beattie, James. *Dissertations, Moral and Critical.* 2 vols. Dublin, 1783.

―――. *Essays.* 3 vols. Philadelphia, 1809.

―――. *Elements of Moral Science.* 2 vols. Philadelphia, 1809.

Blair, Hugh. "Critical Dissertation," in *The Poems of Ossian.* Philadelphia, 1846.

―――. *Lectures on Rhetoric and Belles Lettres.* Philadelphia, 1846.

Burnett, James (Lord Monboddo). *Of the Origin and Progress of Language.* 3 vols. Edinburgh, 1774-76.

Campbell, George. *The Philosophy of Rhetoric.* 2 vols. Edinburgh, 1808.

Dunbar, James. *Essays on the History of Mankind in Rude and Cultivated Ages.* London, 1781.

Ferguson, Adam. *An Essay on the History of Civil Society*. London, 1773.

Fordyce, David. *Elements of Moral Philosophy*, in Robert Dodsley's *The Preceptor*. 2 vols. London, 1748.

Gerard, Alexander. *An Essay on Taste*. Edinburgh, 1780.

————. *An Essay on Genius*. London, 1774.

Gregory, John. *A Comparative View of the State and Faculties of Man, with those of the Animal World*. 8 vols. London, 1774.

Home, Henry (Lord Kames). *Elements of Criticism*. New York, 1838.

————. *Sketches of the History of Man*. 4 vols. Edinburgh, 1778.

Hutcheson, Francis. *An Inquiry into the Original of Our Ideas of Beauty and Virtue*. London, 1725.

————. *An Essay on the Nature and Conduct of the Passions and Affections*. London, 1730.

Ogilvie, John. "An Essay on the Lyric Poetry of the Ancients," in *Poems*. London, 1762.

————. *Philosophical and Critical Observations on the Nature, Character, and Various Species of Compositions*. 2 vols. London, 1774.

Reid, Thomas. *Works*, ed. Sir William Hamilton. 2 vols. Edinburgh, 1863.

Robertson, William. *The History of America*. 3 vols. London, 1821.

Smith, Adam. *The Theory of Moral Sentiments*. London, 1861.

Turnbull, George. *Observations upon Liberal Education*. London, 1742.

SECONDARY SOURCES:

Bryson, Gladys. *Man and Society: The Scottish Inquiry of the Eighteenth Century*. Princeton, N. J., 1945.

Jessop, T. E. *A Bibliography of David Hume and of Scottish Philosophy*. London, 1938.

Jones, Olin McKendree. *Empiricism and Intuitionalism in Reid's Common Sense Philosophy*. Princeton, N. J., 1927.

Laurie, Henry. *Scottish Philosophy in its National Development*. Glasgow, 1902.

Lehmann, W. C. *Adam Ferguson and the Beginnings of Modern Sociology*. New York, 1930.

M'Cosh, J. *The Scottish Philosophy, biographical, expository, critical, from Hutcheson to Hamilton.* New York, 1875.

Pearce, Roy Harvey. "The Eighteenth-Century Scottish Primitivists: Some Reconsiderations," *ELH*, XII (1945), pp. 203-20.

Randall, Helen Whitcomb. *Critical Theory of Lord Kames.* Northampton, Mass., 1949.

Scott, William Robert. *Francis Hutcheson.* Cambridge (England), 1900.

Seth [Pringle-Pattison], A. *Scottish Philosophy.* Edinburgh, 1907.

Snell, John. *The Political Thought of Adam Ferguson.* Wichita, Kansas, 1950.

III. GENERAL REFERENCES

Allen, B. Sprague. *Tides in English Taste (1619-1800).* 2 vols. Cambridge, Mass., 1937.

Bate, Walter Jackson. *From Classic to Romantic, Premises of Taste in Eighteenth-Century England.* Cambridge, Mass., 1946.

Carlyle, Alexander. *Autobiography.* Edinburgh, 1860.

Cassirer, Ernst. *The Philosophy of the Enlightenment.* Princeton, N. J., 1951.

Chandler, F. W. *The Literature of Roguery.* 2 vols. Cambridge (England), 1907.

Crane, Ronald Salmon. "English Criticism: Neo-Classical," in *Dictionary of World Literature,* ed. Joseph T. Shipley. New York, 1943.

————. "Suggestions toward a Genealogy of the 'Man of Feeling,'" *ELH,* I (1934), 205-30.

Dudden, F. Homes. *Henry Fielding.* Oxford, 1952.

Fairchild, Hoxie N. *Religious Trends in English Poetry, 1700-1780.* 2 vols. New York, 1942.

Fitzgerald, Margaret M. *First Follow Nature: Primitivism in English Poetry, 1725-1750.* New York, 1947.

Hazard, Paul. *European Thought in the Eighteenth Century.* New Haven, Conn., 1954.

James, D. G. *The Life of Reason.* London, 1949.

Kaye, F. B., ed. Mandeville's *The Fable of the Bees.* Oxford, 1924.

Lovejoy, Arthur O. *Essays in the History of Ideas.* Baltimore, 1948.

————. *The Great Chain of Being: A Study of the History of an Idea.* Cambridge, Mass., 1950.

McKenzie, Gordon. *Critical Responsiveness: A Study of the Psychological Current in Later Eighteenth-Century Criticism. University of California Publications in English,* vol. XX (1949).

McKillop, Alan Dugald. *The Background of Thomson's Seasons.* Minneapolis, 1942.

Mead, William Edward. *The Grand Tour in the Eighteenth Century.* Boston, 1914.

Monk, Samuel H. *The Sublime: A Study of Critical Theories in XVIII-Century England.* New York, 1935.

Raphael, David Daiches. *The Moral Sense.* Oxford, 1947.

Samson, Ronald Victor. *Progress in the Age of Reason.* Cambridge, Mass., 1956.

Stephen, Leslie. *History of English Thought in the Eighteenth Century.* New York, 1881.

Thompson, Harold William. *A Scottish Man of Feeling: Henry Mackenzie.* London, 1931.

Whitehead, Alfred North. *Science and the Modern World.* New York, 1926.

Whitney, Lois. *Primitivism and the Idea of Progress.* Baltimore, 1934.

Willey, Basil. *The Eighteenth Century Background.* London, 1950.

Woodhouse, A. S. P. "Romanticism and the History of Ideas," in *English Studies Today,* ed. C. L. Wrenn and G. Bullough. Oxford, 1951.

⟨